PUTTING DOWN ROOTS

A history of London's Parks and River

By Pat Morden

Picture research by Stephen Harding

Canadian Cataloguing in Publication Data

Morden, Pat
    Putting down roots

Bibliography: p.
ISBN 0-919549-17-9

1. Thames River (Ont.) - History. 2. Parks - Ontario - London - History. I. Title.

FC3099.L6Z55 1988   971.3'26   C88-095382-9
F1059.5.L6M67 1988

Copyright ©1988 Stonehouse Publications

All rights reserved. No part of this work may be reproduced or transmitted in any form or by any means, electronic or mechanical, including photocopying, recording, or by any information storage and retrieval system, without permission in writing from the publisher.

ISBN 0-919549-17-9
CIP

PRINTED IN CANADA

Published by
Stonehouse Publications
17 Queen Street, St. Catharines, Ontario L2R 5G5
Telephone (416) 684-7251

Cover Illustration

Scene from Springbank Park, 1880
Artist — Henry Nesbitt McAvoy

Courtesy of the London Regional Art Gallery
Gift of Mrs. Jessie Minhinnick, London, Ontario

ACKNOWLEDGEMENTS

I would like to thank the following people for their assistance and support during this project: Maurice Chapman of the P.U.C. for the interview which seeded this book, Glen Curnoe and Mary Velaitis at the London Public Library and Edward Phelps and Guy St-Denis at the Regional Collection, University of Western Ontario, for their assistance in the research; Daniel J. Brock and Ed Phelps for their editorial expertise, freely given; and Barry Fair at the London Regional Art Gallery, for assistance in selecting and copying the cover illustration. In particular, I thank Stephen Harding, who found most of the illustrations used in the book, and copied many of them. His expertise and aesthetic judgement resulted in an interesting and visually appealing group of pictures. A special thank you to Max.

CONTENTS

Dedication
Acknowledgements

1 Introduction
2 "Beautifully Clear": The Thames River in London
3 "A Place of Health and Recreation": Victoria Park
4 "Oh, the Exhiliration Of It": Springbank Park
5 "Great Negligence": The Victoria Boat Disaster
6 "All The Time Rising": Floods in London
7 "Cool, Health-Giving Breezes": London's Lakeside Park
8 London's Parks Under E. V. Buchanan
9 "The Proper Spirit of Play": Sports and Recreation in London Parks
10 Conclusion
11 Bibliography

A Bicycle Club in Victoria Park, 1884. Courtesy, London Historical Museums.

INTRODUCTION

On the east side of the forks, between the main branches of the river Thames, on a regular Eminence about forty feet above the water, is a natural plain, interspersed with small groves of wood, affording in its present state the appearance of a most beautiful park, improved with great cost and taste.

That is how the young D'Arcy Boulton, later Attorney-General of Upper Canada, described the site of London, when he visited the Forks in the first years of the nineteenth century. All of London was once a park, a shady, tree-covered park. Through it ran a lovely sparkling stream.

All that changed when the settlers arrived. Trees were the enemy. They had to be stripped away before the rich soil could be planted. Forests harboured wild animals and cut out the sun. The river was merely a convenient drain.

During the 1830's, London became the "Forest City" — a clearing amongst the trees.

My first impression of it was that of a hamlet or village recently reclaimed from the primeval forest. Everything bore the appearance of recent existence; the openings for the roads, which subsequently became streets, were encumbered with stumps and fragments of trees . . .
(Judge William Elliott, 1837)

More trees were felled and the clearing grew. "The scene presented," wrote a visitor in the 1840's, "is a circuit of several miles of 'cleared' ground, bounded all around by a fence of thick forest." There were stumps everywhere, even in the cellars and kitchens of some houses.

Gradually, Londoners began to want trees again. The stump-filled streets and barren building lots were unattractive, and there was no relief from the hot summer sun. Fewer trees along the riverbanks meant more run-off, and consequently, more severe flooding.

Fortunately for London, James Egan was a farsighted man. Egan began a campaign in 1870 to raise money for a tree-planting campaign. He received enough contributions to enable the city to buy 15,000 25 cent trees from Dorchester and plant them along city streets.

Tree-planting became a London tradition. By 1922, when American town planner Thomas Adams visited the city, he remarked approvingly: "London was described as the stump city in 1842, but today, it properly boasts of the title of forest city."

It was Egan who also had the vision to create London's first park on the dusty parade ground of the old British garrison. Soon there were many parks: some the result of careful planning; some, like Springbank, the happy side-effect of other civic projects; and still others, donations from London's leading citizens. Some parks became peaceful oases, others, busy playgrounds, alive with noise and activity.

Londoners learned to value their river, too. A pure and bright stream when the first settlers arrived, and a cesspool of urban wastes a century later, it is now, once again, the focus of the city's recreational life.

The history of a community is bound up in its pastimes as much as in its business activities, in its natural environment as much as in its man-made environment. London's parks and river are an integral part of the city's past and present.

London, Canada West, by Dr. Darnell, c. 1839
The Artist was standing on what is now Wartley Road, looking northeast

"BEAUTIFULLY CLEAR": THE THAMES RIVER IN LONDON

March 2, 1793: We walked over a rich meadow, and at its extremity came to the forks of the River. The Gov'r wished to examine this situation and its environs, therefore we remained here all day.

He judged it to be a situation eminently calculated for the metropolis of all Canada. Among many other essentials, it possesses the following advantages: Command of territory, internal situation, central position, facility of water communication up and down the Thames . . . the soil is luxuriantly fine; the land rich, capable of being easily cleaned and soon put into a state of agriculture; a pinery upon an adjacent high knoll, other lumber upon the height, well calculated for the erection of public buildings; a climate not inferior to any part of Canada . . .
(Major Littlehale's Diary, 1793)

The river Thames winds its way through London's history, a constant thread, sometimes blue and sometimes a muddy brown, from the earliest days to the present. There would be no London without the river. Without the forks of the river, to be precise. That's where it all started, with a dreamer named John Graves Simcoe.

The river approaches London from the northeast. The north branch flows southwest to Richmond Street, then south to join the south branch at the forks. From there, it flows southwest past Byron, and ultimately, on to Lake St. Clair. There are three large tributaries in the London area. Medway Creek flows from the northwest to converge with the main stream at Richmond Street, and Stoney Creek joins further north. Pottersburg Creek flows into the south branch. When Simcoe first visited London there were many smaller creeks which now flow underground. Carling's Creek, for example, once crossed Richmond Street just south of Oxford Street.

Neutral Indians camped on the flats beside the river they called Askunesippi, the Antlered One, hundreds of years before white men lived in the area. French fur traders called the river La Tranche, the ditch, when they paddled down it to meet Indian trappers. The thick forest bordering the river was home to all kinds of valuable wildlife, including the most important, beaver.

But it was Simcoe who first envisioned a permanent British settlement. Simcoe was an officer in the regular army during the American Revolution. Later he returned to England, married and became involved in politics. In 1791, he was appointed lieutenant-governor of the newly created province of Upper Canada, and he arrived to take up his duties in June 1792. Whatever Simcoe's faults were, he was not a lazy man. In February of 1793, he made an overland trip from Niagara to Detroit, through the heart of his new territory. With him travelled Lieutenant Thomas Talbot, who later settled twenty-nine townships along Lake Erie, and Major Edward Littlehales, whose diary, quoted above, records Simcoe's first sight of the forks.

Simcoe set aside a large piece of land as a Crown Reserve, and began building Dundas Street, the road that was to link his new city with the head of the lake. When one of his surveyors suggested that a system of locks on the river would render it navigable as far as the forks, Simcoe incorporated the suggestion in his plans.

But in 1796 Simcoe left Upper Canada and never returned. York (later Toronto) became the provincial capital and the Crown Reserve at the forks of the Thames remained in its virgin state.

In 1804, when Lord Selkirk passed along the river on the way to his ill-fated Baldoon settlement, he too admired the location that had so taken Simcoe's fancy, but he noted ironically that "one Chippaway Bark Whigwham" was all the "great City of London" contained.

The river increases in beauty as it goes down. The water is beautifully clear on a gravel bottom . . . Left our encampment and stopt a few minutes at the Forks, in the great City of London, where there is one Chippaway Bark Whigwham . . .
(Lord Selkirk's Diary, June 1804)

Not long after Selkirk's visit, London's first settler, Joshua Applegarth, arrived to take up a land grant, on the condition that he grow hemp to make rope for the British navy. Applegarth did not stay, but by the 1820's, other settlers were beginning to trickle into both Westminster and London Townships.

Settlement began to move more swiftly in 1826, when London was chosen as the new district capital (to replace Vittoria, where the district courthouse had just burned down) and the townsite was surveyed. The river remained very important. When the castle-like Courthouse was designed, the main entrance was on the river side. The Courthouse square became the centre of the settlement.

One of the town's first large houses (now "Eldon House", a city museum) was built by John Harris, treasurer of the London District, on a hill overlooking the river, 200 yards north of the Courthouse. When the British garrison was established in London after the Rebellion of 1837, the officers were often entertained by the Harris daughters. It is easy to imagine the girls and their escorts strolling arm in arm through the gardens to enjoy the beauty of the view.

A few years later, other members of London's elite chose riverside locations for their houses. In 1845, Henry Becher built "Thornwood" (now 329 St. George Street) overlooking the north branch, and Elijah Leonard, Junior moved into "Locust Mount" (661

Talbot Street) in 1854.

The first bridge across the Thames was built at the foot of York Street in 1826, but a ferry service had operated nearby at an even earlier date. Blackfriars Bridge was constructed next, in 1831.

Referring to old Blackfriars Bridge it may be of interest to note that during the rebellion of '37 sentinels were posted at either end, and no one was allowed to pass who could not give the countersign. The humor of this lies in the fact that at that particular time the water was so low that the riverbed could be crossed dry-shod
(Illustrated London, *Archie Bremner.)*

Other bridges followed at Wellington and Ridout Streets. The first Ridout Street bridge, built in 1848, was an impressive suspension bridge anchored by two heavy stone abutments. Unfortunately for the residents of Westminster, the suburb across the river, who had hoped that the bridge would raise property values, it was less sturdy than it appeared.

In fact, the thing was just constructed, the elegant structure emerged as a whole into being (lots rose immensely — 10 pounds per foot was laughed at) when down came sailing on the surface of the river a slight puff of wind, when over toppled the ''elegant structure'' (village lots also fell considerably) into the mocking river below. . . .
(London Free Press, *February 24, 1862)*

According to one story, the disaster was due to the fact that the men who had driven the piles for the bridge had made their work easier by sawing off the tops of the piles at night.

In fact, it was common for the early wooden bridges to collapse or be damaged by flooding. London's first two iron bridges were built in 1875. One of these, Blackfriars, still arches elegantly across the river.

The importance of bridges to the early citizens of the city is illustrated by a petition, reportedly eight feet long, presented by a group of citizens to persuade City council to build a bridge at Oxford Street. The petition read:

We the undersigned residents and ratepayers of the county of Middlesex respectfully draw the attention of your honourable body to the necessity that exists for the erection of a bridge on the second concession of London Township, across the river Thames, connecting the village of London West with the city of London at Oxford Street, that the erection of the said bridge would be a great benefit to a very large number of the inhabitants of the county, living to the west and northwest of the city of London as it would render a safe approach all seasons from the county to the city, without any of the natural obstructions that now exist . . .
(Petition presented to Middlesex County Council, June 1881)

Blackfriars Bridge, one of the first iron bridges in London, c. 1880. Carling's Brewery in the background.

From Carling's Brewery (at left) looking south toward Blackfriar's Bridge, c. 1880.

The inhabitants of London West were ready, if necessary, to defray part of the cost of the bridge by private subscription. In December 1881 the bridge was approved by council and by January, the project was finished. There are now eighteen bridges over the Thames in London, as well as 15 smaller bridges over the tributaries.

There have been mills along the Thames since the eighteenth century. One of the first in London was Blackfriars grist mill, built in c. 1834. Thomas Water's mill, located where Carling's Creek entered the Thames (now the end of Anne Street) was built at about the same time. Water's Mill was a favourite bathing spot for the British soldiers, although there were several drownings as a result of the unpredictable cold springs in the river at that point. Charles Hunt's City Mills was constructed in 1854 on the south branch, close by Labatt's Brewery. The mill was water-powered until 1917, when Hunt's moved to an East London location. The mill dam was a popular swimming spot until it collapsed in 1935. Cherry Mills was located at the foot of St. James Street by the 1850s.

Many Londoners remember Saunby's Mill, on the north branch opposite Gibbon's Park. A woolen mill was built on the site in the 1840s, and a grist mill was added in c. 1857. During the 1860s, both mills were bought by William Hilliard and J.D. Saunby. The mills were operated by T. Dexter and Son from 1899 until 1938. Converted to various uses, including, during the late 1930's, a dance hall, Saunby's Mill survived until a major fire in 1983.

As London grew, it spread to the east, away from the banks of the Thames. By the 1850s, industrial and commercial activity began to cluster around the railway lines. The river remained the centre of London's recreational activities.

After the exciting and profitable discovery of oil near Petrolia during the late 1850s, a well was drilled at the forks. It was not black gold that gushed forth, however, but sulphur water. Undeterred, an American entrepreneur, Charles Dunnett, opened a health spa, known as Ontario White Sulphur Springs, which operated until 1906. The beneficial waters, Dunnett claimed, were good for rhuematism, gout, scrofula, dyspepsia, nervous prostration, and "Female Diseases". American millionaire Cornelius Vanderbilt believed the claims. He arrived in 1869 to take the waters and, apparently rejuvenated, married his eighteen-year-old fiance in the Tecumseh Hotel. The city maintained a drinking fountain of sulphur water on the site of Dunnett's enterprise for many years.

Every winter large blocks of ice were cut from the river. Covered in sawdust and stored in cool cellars, the ice was kept until the following summer, providing the only refrigeration available. Artificial ice-making equipment was introduced in the 1880s, and the ice harvest ceased.

All kinds of boating flourished on the river. In 1880, Ned Hanlan, the famous Canadian sculler, attended a regatta on the Thames.

Hunt's City Mills, with millstream in foreground, c. 1930.

The Sulphur Springs, at the Forks of the Thames, c. 1870.

Fancy the river dotted with innumerable row boats, the balconies of Springbank Hotel crowded, the bank on the north shore hidden by ladies and gentlemen, the steamers lying along the shores loaded to the utmost capacity, every tree along the course shading its quiet group underneath, and one has the scene in his mind.
(London Free Press, *July 9, 1880)*

Professional and amateur races were held, and although Hanlan was not a competitor, he did some exhibition sculling for the enthusiastic crowd.

But most boating on the river was non-competitive. In 1881, William Judson and a friend sailed down the Thames from London to the mouth of the river. Judson later published his wry, and sometimes lyrical, account of the trip. Here is how he described the Thames through London:

On a lovely morning in June the Number Thirteen (Judson's boat) pulled out under the shadow of Kensington Bridge into the sunlight and ripple and sparkle of a pic-nic day on the Thames.

Crossing the "Forks", "where brook and river meet", and rounding into the channel, the sail was set to a fair breeze from the north, and our tiny vessel joined a stream of fancy craft which hurried with steam, sail, oars or paddle, to the rendez-vous of the day.

For London is famed, or should be, for its fancy craft — not to mention some much beflagged steamers of peculiar patterns, screaming at each other and the passengers . . . There were yawls, scows, dug-outs, bark canoes, shells, tubs and kayaks, besides scores of skiffs, light, strong and graceful as one need wish . . .

On Kensington Flats cattle were gathering in the shadows of huge sycamores, or cooling their feet in the shallow marge of the stream, which reflected everything like a mirror . . . Under the long bridge we went, and into the cove, where a party of young people were gathering water lilies. No one should ever pass the cove in June without looking, for water lilies are then at their best. In thousands they lay like stars of silver on the blue firmament of quiet water, glowing against the dark green of lily pads, and flashing into lines of pure white and tender green as they receded into the hazy distance. Just a look, and off again by the foot of Mount Pleasant . . . by picturesque huts, a little rustic bridge, under the spruce shadows of Woodland Park . . . **(Kuhleborn**, *by "Professor Blot" (William Judson), 1881)*

It was in September 1878 that the "Forest City", London's first paddlewheel steamer, began operating a regular service along the lovely route Judson described, from the forks to the new municipal waterworks (now Springbank Park). The story of the steamer excursions and their tragic end is told in a later chapter.

For several years after the accident, boating on the river was unpopular. Eventually the horror faded. By the turn of the century, the London Boat Club, which has existed sice the 1850s, was flourishing again, offering docking facilities at the forks, as well as a golf course and bowling green.

Archie Bremner, writing in 1897, rhapsodized over the beauties of the river at the forks: "A feature of London, preserved by no other city, is the proximity to the business center of the most charming scenery — delightful landscapes, sylvan glades, purling streams and pellucid ponds."

That idyllic picture was soon to change.

There had always been industry on the river. The Leonard foundry was located on Fullarton Street, right opposite "Eldon House", until 1865. Labatt's brewery was not far away on the south branch, and a soap factory opened up river from Labatt's in 1860. The Dennis Wire and Iron Company had opened a plant at the forks by 1870.

By 1918, the city, in the grip of a post-war depression, actively encouraged Penmans textile factory to locate at the forks. When taxed by a concerned citizen, Mayor C.R. Somerville reportedly replied: "The city has no aesthetic taste as you know. It is like a corporation; it has no soul."

When American town planner Thomas Adams visited the city in 1922, he wrote in his report to the city officials:

I have previously referred to the beauties that London enjoys in having the River Thames running through it. The city should not allow building of any kind on lands subject to flood and should acquire as many of these lands as possible for additional playgrounds and parkways . . . More care should be taken to prevent dumping of refuse on the banks of the River.
("Report on Town Planning Survey of the City of London, *April-May 1922", Thomas Adams)*

It was not only the riverbanks, but the water itself that had suffered from years of neglect. Untreated sewage and industrial wastes had been pumped into the river and its tributaries since the beginning of settlement. Lord Tweedsmuir, visiting London in the 1940s, urged E.V. Buchanan, manager of the P.U.C. to clean up the river, adding that he hoped they would be able to go fishing together by the next time he visited the city.

The Depression and World War Two intervened before anything could be done, In 1945, the city formulated a 25-year riverbank acquisition and beautification plan, but there was little money available to carry it out. Water quality continued to be a major concern. A 1952 report on the Upper Thames Valley asserted:

The city of London is potentially the most serious source of pollution on the watershed. Large-scale disposal facilities have been in operation for many years but these are now overloaded . . . Both branches of the river are heavily polluted at London, and the river below London is also foul.
(Upper Thames Valley Conservation Report, *1952)*

A clean-up program was launched, but took some years to show results. It is unlikely that the Thames will ever recover the crystal clarity that Lord Selkirk noted in 1804.

In 1960, the city retained a Toronto engineering firm, A.D. Margison and Associates, to study and suggest remedies for London's traffic problems. The engineers suggested a network of expressways built along the open floodplain land of the Thames river valley. Fortunately, this plan was never put into effect. Instead, the city joined with the Upper Thames River Conservation Authority to begin a major river bank acquisition program. By 1986, the city owned 800 acres of parkland along the river.

At the forks, the Dennisteel (formerly Dennis Wire and Steel) factory was bought by the city and demolished in 1964. In 1975, the Westview Apartments was acquired and cleared, and within two years, the old Penman's factory and other commercial buildings had disappeared.

When the new courthouse was built on the northeast corner of Dundas and Ridout streets, a group of citizens came up with a scheme to use the old courthouse as an arts and entertainment centre, surrounded by the newly cleared parkland. Another, equally committed, group wanted to build a new art gallery on the Dennisteel site. After long and acrimonious debate, the art gallery was built, and the old courthouse became the Middlesex County Building, administrative centre of the county. A small park was created on the river below the old jail, and Harris Park was developed below "Eldon House". During the early 70s, riverboat cruises from the forks to Springbank Park began again.

Today, the river is once again the centre of London recreation. Bike and hiking paths extend along both branches of the river, linking a series of public parks and natural areas. The most recent development at the forks itself is the Peace Garden, installed in 1987.

Would Simcoe recognize the forks, site of his "metropolis of all Canada", today? Possibly not. But at least he would still find green meadows running down to the water's edge, and a beauty that Londoners are beginning to appreciate again.

Advertisement card for Sulphur Springs pool, no date.

"A PLACE OF HEALTH AND RECREATION": VICTORIA PARK

Beyond the charmed oasis of the park, where the heaviest vehicular traffic is the prams, the city plows noisily on its way: the buses bang and rattle; the car gears grind and scream. But in the park the sounds are of voices, and feet deadened on the sod, and children calling, and the throbbing of the music of the band, the high melody of the fiddle or the sound of the trumpet and the flute. Verdi, perhaps, or Strauss, or a brisk polka to set older feet jiggling a little. The music comes out of the bandshell and flows over the park, as the colored water in the fountain sends bright showers into the dusk.
(**London Free Press**, *August 4, 1952*)

Victoria Park was not always as peaceful as it was on that evening in 1952.

Instead of 'feet deadened on the sod and children calling', there was once the tramp of marching feet and the hoarse shouting of orders. At one time, the music was distinctly military. Victoria Park began life as part of the British garrison, established in London in 1838.

In December 1837, Upper Canada was torn apart by rebellion. William Lyon Mackenzie led an abortive assault on Toronto, while Dr. Charles Duncombe organized a gathering of disaffected farmers in the Brantford area. Mackenzie and some of the other rebels fled to the United States, where they, with American allies, organized border raids which continued throughout 1838. London, because of its central position, was chosen as the site of a new British garrison to guard against attack from the south. Jane O'Brien, wife of Dennis O'Brien, one of London's first businessmen, wrote to a friend in Nova Scotia in May 1838:

London since December last has been one continual scene of confusion, crowded with soldiers, and large numbers were billeted on each house for want of barracks, and it has been but recently since we got rid of them: and arrests of persons suspected of being implicated in the outbreak were going on through the winter, and among the number was my brother-in-law . . . Mr. O'Brien is well. He has escaped censure from all parties, and has done a great amount of business with the Government and has gotten nearly all his money. He has rented his brick buildings for barracks.
(quoted in **Illustrated London**, *Archie Bremner*)

Mr. O'Brien's 'brick buildings' continued as barracks until 1843. Meanwhile, a military reserve was established, bounded by Queens Avenue, Waterloo, Clarence and Kenneth (just south of Piccadilly) Streets. On the land that is now Victoria Park, more barracks were erected and a space was cleared for a parade ground.

The British officers quickly became an essential part of the town's social life, as this little verse, said to be written by a young officer, attests:

*Sing the delights of London society —
Epaulette, sabretache, sword-knot, and plume;
Always enchanting, yet knows no variety —
Scarlet alone can embellish a room.
Flirting and chattering,
Bend the proud heroes that fight for the crown:
Dancing cotillions,
Cutting civilians,
These are the joys of a garrison town.*
(quoted in **The Diary of Charlotte Harris**)

Ordinary citizens enjoyed the spectacle of scarlet tunics, too. They flocked to the garrison's military display held annually in May in honour of the Queen's birthday. Cricket matches on the parade ground also attracted good crowds.

The soldiers were kept busy through the years of peace with civilian tasks. They cleared many of the stumps from London streets and used them to build a fence around their parade grounds. As fatigue duty, Colonel Horn of the 20th regiment ordered his men to level a 30-foot hill between Hyman and Pall Mall Streets and use the earth to dam Carling's Creek — Lake Horn was the result. The soldiers bathed and even boated in the lake they had created.

The stump fence became the subject of a bitter controversy between the civilian population and the soldiers. According to an old story, the fence enclosed the pie-shaped piece of land between Richmond and Clarence Streets, known as the Gore. The citizens of London asked that the stumps be removed from that portion, not strictly part of the military reserve. The military authorities refused, so a team of intrepid civilians marched in to do the job themselves. Blank artillery shells were fired over their heads while they worked, with the result that several of the stumps were set on fire. The barracks fire engine was called out to douse the flames.

The British garrison was finally withdrawn in 1868 and the barracks and drill square were left to moulder. The barracks soon became very run-down: ". . . a resort of characters of the worst sort." Fortunately, they burned down in 1873.

About this time, several prominent Londoners began to agitate for public parks.

London had a park as early as 1846. Colonel Mahlon Burwell, the surveyor who laid out London's townsite, bequeathed a piece of land south of Stanley Street, between Wharncliffe and Wortley Roads, to the city as a recreation ground. It was to be called St. James Park.

But London was still a pioneer town. Council decided that it could not afford to maintain the land as a park and leased it to Mr. Thomas Francis, the former City Inspector, on the condition that he plant trees on the property. Francis planted only potatoes. In 1861, a committee of Council decided to re-lease the

View from Cricket Square (now Victoria Park) showing pine stump fence, 1860.

land to a Mr. Coleman, once again on the condition that trees be planted, but Francis proved a hard tenant to dislodge.

Coleman, on Friday last, went to Mr. Francis and demanded possession; Mr. Francis refused, whereupon Coleman lost his temper, threatened to kill Francis and finally broke the lock off the gate and took forcible possession.
(**London Free Press**, *April 22, 1861*)

Coleman was fined $4.00 and costs as a result, and the city, perhaps feeling that parks were more trouble than they were worth, later sold off St. James Park for building lots.

By the late 1860s, however, the city had grown. There were fewer open spaces. The trees which had once grown so thickly were almost gone. In 1868, in response to public pressure, the grounds of the Courthouse were granted for a park. Trees were planted, but perhaps because many Londoners remembered attending public executions nearby, the space was little used.

In 1871, a Standing Committee on Public Parks was set up by City Council at the instigation of Alderman James Egan, with the support of John Carling.

In 1873, Egan went to Ottawa to ask for title to a portion of the old military reserve for a park. He hoped to obtain forty acres north of Central Avenue, including Carling's Creek and Lake Horn. Instead, he received the thirteen acres that are now Victoria Park.

When it was suggested that the land Egan had obtained be used as building lots instead of parkland,

Carling spoke eloquently in favour of the park proposal.

It was not merely the city of today that they should look to but to the city it was likely to become 40 or 50 years hence . . . Let us go to work and provide an expansive pleasure ground, a breathing place for the citizens, where they and their children may assemble and breathe purer air.
(**London Free Press**, *December 19, 1873*)

In August 1874, Lord Dufferin, the Governor General, visited London and formally dedicated Victoria Park. In his speech, he compared old and new London, and surprisingly, found much in favour of the new one:

While in certain respects you are behind, in others you are infinitely superior to Old London. You do not have the poor of London . . . the foul air of London, its miserable alleys, where heaps of human kind are crowded together . . . Neither are your streets polluted by those disgraceful evidences of vice and destitution by which I regret to say the streets of the British capital are contaminated . . . Here at all event, no matter how humble may be the circumstances of any citizen, he can enjoy fresh air and decent accommodation and above everything else, there is open to him, provided he be sober and industrious, the prospect of improving his position . . .
(**London Free Press**, *August 28, 1874*)

His words were greeted with a rousing three cheers, and Shanly's Battery, a militia unit, fired off a ceremonial salute. According to the **Free Press**: "The park will be a place of Health and Recreation not only for the present generation but for many more to come."

In March 1878, master gardener William Miller was persuaded to come to London and lay out the new park. Miller was head gardener at Fairmont Park in Philadelphia and had designed the grounds for the U.S. Centennial Exposition at Philadelphia two years earlier. There was, inevitably, some controversy over Miller's plan; some members of city council insisted that a local gardener be used for the project.

A total of 331 trees and 72 shrubs were planted, adding to the double row of maple trees which already surrounded the grounds. In 1879, an elaborate ornamental fountain topped by a cupid was added. Three guns, one British and two Russian, brought to London from Sevastopol by John Carling in 1860, were placed in the park. A lily pond, an essential item in any Victorian park, was added later.

Londoners did not immediately grasp the meaning of this new piece of open land. There were frequent complaints that cows, pigs and geese were allowed to graze on it. A high picket fence was erected to remedy the situation, but the fence itself became unsightly and was removed.

In the end, however, the idea caught on. By the early 1880's, the **Free Press** could report with pride:

A Park has been planned, levelled, sodded and laid out in a tasty manner; and what was once a barren barrack ground is now in summertime made bright and beautiful by the flowers and trees and shrubs which flourish and bloom therein. This is one of the many changes which illustrate the increasing wealth of the city and the demand for luxury, under which heading a place of resort of this character must be classed. Parks are only to be found in growing towns and cities . . .

(**London Free Press**, *January 3, 1882*)

The Fountain at Victoria Park, c. 1880.

The Fish pond at Victoria Park, c. 1890.

If parks were a sign of growth and prosperity, then London was prospering. The same year that Victoria received its fountain, Queen's Park was dedicated.

In 1878, a group of citizens asked that Salter's Grove, a beautiful woodland just east of the city, be made into a park. They even took up a subscription to defray the costs. The subscription book, still preserved in the P.U.C. archives, reads:

We the undersigned hereby agree to pay to Benjamin Cronyn, W.H. Birrell and Andrew McCormick who have been appointed the Public Park Committee, the sums written herein after our respective names for the purpose of fencing and laying out Salter's Grove as a Public Park for the City of London.
London, 24 April, 1879

A large bandstand was erected, spruce trees were planted and a two hundred yard track was laid out. The following year, the park was used for a sports program on the May 24th holiday. Such competitions as the Greasy Pig Race and Climbing the Greasy Pole were held, and in the evening the band of the 7th Fusiliers played for dancing. The **Free Press** reported:

No place could be better adapted for a demonstration of this kind than Queen's Park, affording as it does a quiet and cool retreat for those who do not desire to participate in the games and plenty of space for races, ball-playing, etc....
(**London Free Press**, *May 25, 1880*)

In 1887, the Western Fair Association purchased the park to be used as the fair grounds. The beautiful stands of pine trees were cut down to make way for a new exhibition building and other facilities. While Victoria Park, an oasis of green, was created from a barren parade ground, Queen's Park, once a natural beauty spot, became increasingly barren.

Victoria Park was one of the first public places in London to be lit with electricity. Seven thousand people attended the lighting-up in 1882.

... Five large lamps on high poles illuminated the grounds in a manner that excited admiration, everything within the radiance of the light being rendered as distinct and as clear as in daylight ...
(**London Free Press**, *June 12, 1882*)

The magic of Victoria Park inspired a popular song. In the summer of 1891, Cy Warman, a railway man and poet, was visiting his sweetheart, Myrtle Marie Jones, a student at the Academy of the Sacred Heart (on the site of Catholic Central Highschool). One evening after walking Marie back to the school, Warman strolled into Victoria Park, sat down on a park bench and composed "Sweet Marie".

It's a secret in my heart, Sweet Marie,
A tale I would impart, love to thee,
Every daisy in the dell
Knows my secret, knows it well
And yet I dare not tell, Sweet Marie.

Victoria Park with the Provincial Exhibition Building in the background, c. 1875

The words were set to music by Raymond Moore and the song became very popular. Warman married his sweet Marie and built a large house in North London where they lived for many years.

The park's large squirrel population is not indigenous; it originated with the purchase of four pairs of squirrels in 1914. Others were added in subsequent years.

Victoria Park's military connections continued long past the days of the British garrison. In 1912, the Duke of Connaught unveiled the Soldier's Monument, a memorial honouring the dead of the Boer War by Montreal sculptor George W. Hill. Various delays had plagued its construction, including a fire at the quarry which destroyed the pedestal. Even the unveiling was not trouble free.

Grasping an end of rope he gave a slight pull and part of the red, white and blue draping loosened at the top of the monument and displayed to the wondering gaze of many the top of the soldier's head. The sheet caught on the arms and it was necessary to get a pole and loosen the folds but as the whole covering fell and one of the handsomest monuments in Canada stood revealed to thousands of eyes, a lusty cheer for the royal party and for the heroes who died on a battlefield many thousands of miles away, rang out.
(**London Free Press**, *May 30, 1912*)

At the end of World War One, thousands of Londoners again crowded into Victoria Park, this time to watch the Kaiser burned in effigy. Some years later, members of the Imperial Order of the Daughters of the Empire decided that a war memorial should be erected. Plans for the cenotaph in Whitehall, London, England were purchased from the architect, Sir Edward Lutyens, in 1929, and an exact replica of the memorial was unveiled on November 10, 1934.

In 1939, the original fountain was replaced by an elaborate new one, illuminated with coloured lights. There were traffic jams on the park drive as motorists sat transfixed by the new marvel, but Arthur Ford, editor of the **Free Press**, thought it "hideous". In 1951 the drives were narrowed and the park was closed to motor traffic.

Victoria Park has been famous for its band concerts for well over one hundred years. In June 1881, the Free Press reported:

Victoria Park presented a gratifying spectacle the which we should desire to see often repeated. On that occasion, as on many others, the band played from a large round wooden bandstand in the centre of the park. It was from the same platform that the Prince of Wales, later King Edward the Eighth, greeted thousands of Londoners during his 1919 visit.

Never in the history of the city did Victoria Park hold such a crowd as wildly acclaimed the prince as he smilingly mounted the steps to the bandstand. Twenty thousand people cheered in a deafening roar. The sound of the band was

lost in the applause. The prince took off his hat and waved it, a happy smile on his face, at the 12,000 school kiddies who were massed east of the stand.
(**London Advertiser**, *October 23, 1919*)

The old wooden structure was past its prime by the 1930s. The Kiwanis Club of London began collecting donations for a new one, but because of war-time restrictions on building materials, had to wait until the end of the war to complete the project. In the meantime, a temporary structure was raised so that servicemen on leave could be entertained with concerts and sing-a-longs. The Kiwanis bandshell was officially opened June 26, 1950. Old-fashioned band concerts, rock concerts, movies, musicals and plays, civic receptions, Dominion Day and Centennial celebrations — the bandshell has served London well. It has also been the main stage of the Home County Folk Festival, held in the park every July since 1974.

One Victoria Park tradition which has now lapsed was the annual carpet flower bed at the southwest corner of the park. Each year for over thirty-five years it was planted in a different design by Ted Foster, who retired as superintendant of parks in 1957. In 1945, a Welcome Home design incorporated emblems of the army, navy and air force as a tribute to returning servicemen. A more permanent tribute is the "Holy Roller", a tank used on the beaches of Normandy in 1944, which now stands sentinel on the north side of the park.

There has been a skating rink at the park since 1913. On December 5, 1958, the lights were switched on for the first Winter Wonderland, a display of coloured lights and seasonal displays that has become part of Christmas for many London children.

Victoria Park is truly the heart of downtown London. Perhaps that is why it has aroused such strong feelings in recent years. In 1986, when Ploughshares London suggested Victoria as the site for a Peace Garden, veterans' groups protested vehemently, pointing out the long historical connections between the park and the military. In the end, the Peace Garden was transferred to the forks of the Thames.

More recently, the P.U.C., recognizing the need to refurbish some of the park's amenities, came up with a plan for major changes, including a sunken amphitheatre to replace the bandshell, a "Victorian teahouse", a snack bar, and information kiosks. Londoners reacted with an emphatic 'no'. According to one letter-writer: "London is so fortunate to have an old-fashioned, restful oasis of greenery in such a central location that it would be criminal to change it."

Sir John Carling would have been proud.

Victoria Park, c. 1910.

"OH, THE EXHILARATION OF IT": SPRINGBANK PARK

One afternoon, Alderman James Egan, John Carling and a number of other men whose names are famous in London, were holding a picnic across the river from the present site of the waterworks park at Springbank. The idea occurred to Egan as he looked at Coombe's mill and the great hill, and thought of the abundant springs, that the top of the hill would be an ideal place for a reservoir, and its base for the waterworks plant. A couple of years later, the inspiration was turned to good account.
(**London Advertiser**, *July 20, 1917*)

To very good account, most Londoners would agree. Alderman Egan's inspiration led to the creation of the city waterworks and its most popular attraction — Springbank Park.

For many years, Londoners got water from their own private wells, or used public ones. The quality of the water was unreliable, as the typhoid epidemic of 1847 attests. During the 1850s, a waterworks company was formed to bring water from the Westminster ponds, but the scheme foundered when it was discovered that the ponds contained only surface water.

Water was also needed to fight fires. Large wooden tanks were built in various parts of the city and filled with water to supply the pumps of the fire brigade. The **Free Press**, however, was not impressed by this measure:

It is true that a few tanks have been placed at remote intervals which form admirable receptacles for gravel and dirt of all kinds, but they are entirely useless in case of fire. The London people hesitate about having water works while the present tanks leak at a rate of three feet in a single night. There is no wonder the place doesn't prosper.
(*Quoted in* **The Story of London's Water Supply**, *E.V. Buchanan*)

In spite of the strong words, London ratepayers soundly defeated a waterworks proposal in 1875. The measure was finally passed in 1877. The **London Advertiser**, which opposed the scheme editorially, commented caustically: ". . . another scheme for waterworks, bountifully sprinkled with religion and politics, but hastily considered and extravagant in its aims . . . was carried."

A dam was built on the river so that water could be used to power the pump, which was housed in an attractive cottage-style building. Spring water was pumped from collecting ponds to the reservoir at the top of Hungerford Hill. From there, gravity was used to feed it to the thirsty city. The entire system was built by William Robinson, city engineer and noted architect, at a cost of under $400,000. When John Carling came to write the first annual report of the Board of Water Commissioners in 1879, he was clearly well pleased with the work completed.

It is unnecessary to state here what all are now convinced of, that in no town or city on this continent is there to be found a supply of purer and more wholesome water.
(*Annual Report of the Board of Water Commissioners, 1878*)

The city continued to buy land in the vicinity of the waterworks until, by 1911, it owned almost 400 acres.

As pleased as Londoners were to have a safe water supply, it was an added bonus that the waterworks property was such a scenic spot. Before long, it had become a popular resort, serviced by river steamers. An old building beside the pumphouse became a pavilion where refreshments could be purchased, and an observatory was built on one of the hills. A Toronto newspaper man, who visited the observatory in 1879, reported:

The view at this season is really magnificent; on the east city spires peer through the tops of the trees and on the west is a glorious view of hill and dale the one a thin dividing silver streak running far away into the wooded slopes until it is lost to view.
(*quoted in "Looking Over Western Ontario",* **London Free Press**, *Aug. 1, 1979*)

An excursion to the waterworks property, or Chestnut Park as it was called, was an all-day outing. It began by walking or riding to the docks at the river forks, and waiting for passage on one of the steamers. At the park, a brisk walk to the observatory, or perhaps a turn on the dance floor of the pavilion, sharpened the appetite for a substantial Victorian picnic. One nineteenth century cookbook suggested this menu for a party of twenty:

    5 lbs. of Cold Salmon
    1 Quarter of Lamb with Mint Sauce
    8 lbs. Pickled Brisket of Beef
    1 Tongue
    1 Galantine of Veal
    1 Chicken Pie
    Salad and Dressing
    2 Fruit Tarts
    2 doz. Cheesecakes
    2 Creams
    2 Jellies
    4 Loaves of Bread
    2 lbs. of Biscuits
    1 1/2 lbs. of Cheese
    6 lbs. of Strawberries
(**Mrs. Beeton's Book of Household Management**, *1897*)

Thousands of Londoners made the trip — until May 24, 1881. The "Victoria" accident put an end to steamer travel on the river. As a result, the popularity of the waterworks grounds declined. It could still be reached by carriage, and later by horse-drawn bus, along the rough and dusty Pipeline Road, but many

Official Opening of London Waterworks at Springbank, 1878.

The Pavilion at Springbank, c. 1896.

Londoners preferred the more pleasant rail trip to Port Stanley.

By the 1890s, interest in Springbank revived. In 1892, the Board of Water Commissioners began to make improvements, and over the next two years stumps and brush were removed from around Reservoir Hill, paths were laid out and gravelled, shade trees planted, and benches and swings built. Just to the east of the park, Wonderland, described in 1878 as a "beautiful sylvan retreat", was developed by Captain C. M. Foster, owner of a pleasure boat business, into a small resort with a dance hall.

By 1895, the London Street Railway began negotiating for the right to run their line through the Springbank grounds. Agreement was reached in 1896, and service began on May 25. According to the **Free Press**, 10 to 12,000 Londoners were carried to the park that day by streetcar, but the cars were over-crowded and delayed. Despite start-up problems, the street railway service meant that the park was more accessible than it had ever been. The trip itself, in open-sided cars, was an event:

Measured by the chain, it is six miles to Springbank Park.

Counted by the time required to make the round trip, it is one hour.

Gauged by the pleasure of the thing, it is a hornpipe of joy, it is intoxication.

To the youth and lady-love it is an imperial chariot, drawn by the cherubim and seraphim of laughter and song . . .

Smiling meadows and laughing gardens, luxurious in the sunlight, nod a how-d'-do.

Life opens the hamper of purest ozone, and the nerves tingle and jingle with renewed vigour.

The vision wanders afar and feasts on the glory of distant landscape.

The trolley hums a peaceful lay, rolling smoothly, cheerfully parkwards.

The sparkling waters of the ponds look up and give a passing notice. This is the Park.

Oh, the exhilaration of it!

(**"Souvenir of Springbank Park"**, *1902*)

Moonlight excursions, which had once been popular on the river steamers, became a feature of the street railway service. The tracks and the grounds were electrically lit, creating a romantic setting. Streetcars continued to operate between downtown London and Springbank until 1935.

In 1897, an open air theatre was built at the park, offering afternoon and evening performances for 15 and 25 cents. The original pavilion burned down that year and a new, larger one, complete with a gingerbread-trimmed tower, was built.

The Board of Water Commissioners continued to make improvements. A permanent gardener was hired in 1906, and tennis and bowling lawns were laid out west of the pavilion in 1907. In 1912, a Parks Department was formed and a consultant prepared a ten year plan for London's parks. The first step was the reconstruction of the entrances and roads at Springbank.

In 1914, three raccoons and three owls were purchased to form the nucleus of a zoo at Springbank. It soon had a variety of animals, including deer, brown bears, bison, and even an elk. In 1934, E.V. Buchanan wrote: ". . . the zoo is a never-ending source of interest and education to old and young alike."

It was also in 1914 that a municipal camp ground was established at Wonderland. In 1922 it was converted into a motor camp:

London's Motor Camp at Wonderland is the outdoors quest chamber for the hundreds of camping tourists who

A stroll through Springbank Park, c. 1900.

The Look-out at Reservoir Hill, c. 1905.

Picnicking by the Pavilion, Springbank, c. 1900.

A streetcar in front of the pumphouse at Springbank Park, 1906.

Riverbank above the pumphouse, Springbank Park, c. 1900.

reach the Heart of Ontario in their summer wanderings, and every convenience, from electric cooking stoves to pure Springbank water, is provided for the visitors.
(**P.U.C. Annual Report**, *1923*)

The sudden influx of servicemen provided the impetus for the Springbank Amusement Park, which opened in 1914. According to a 1919 newspaper report:

The Amusement Park though separate from Springbank is practically a part of it. When the car stops opposite the big pavilion, you can step immediately into the Amusement Park without any cost to you . . . Here ice cream and cooling drinks of the purest kinds can be partaken of in the utmost comfort and amidst the most pleasant surroundings.

In addition to the popular amusement devices of last year — the cannon ball coaster, the merry-go-round, the bowling alleys, etc. — some new ones have been installed. Among these is 'The House of Mirth' . . . in which you go through a laughable but perfectly safe experience . . .
(**The Echo**, *May 22, 1919*)

A few years later, a jitney dance hall, with sides which could be raised to admit cool breezes, was built. The patrons paid five cents per dance to sway to the music of, amongst others, the Johnny Downs orchestra. The Springbank dance hall continued to be popular throughout the Second World War, but burned down in 1946.

In 1920, a new attraction was added to Springbank. Mrs. Sarah Stevenson, inspired by a visit to an American park with a miniature train, ordered one for Springbank. She hired James Kennedy, an Irishman with experience on full-size trains, as engineer, and began a tradition which has persisted to the present. When she died in 1944, a **Free Press** reporter wrote:

Love of children was her incentive in building the well-known Springbank concession, and she could hardly wait until it could be completed so that she could watch the children have their first rides . . . Every day of the 22 seasons her train has been running, Mrs. Stevenson would be at Springbank Park, selling tickets, watching over the children, making sure that none were hurt, and that all who could got a ride. Once a child rode on the train, Mrs. Stevenson hardly every forgot him, remembering the children as they came to the park year after year . . .
(**London Free Press**, *March 25, 1944*)

Buffaloes at Springbank Zoo, 1921. According to one story, a visitor to the park was once gored by one of these animals, and sued the city for damages.

Jimmie Kennedy married Sarah Stevenson's daughter, Florence. After his mother-in-law's death, he and Florence ran the train for another 22 years. When he retired in 1965, the train was bought by Supertest and given to the Central London Lion's Club to run. It proved difficult to find an engineer to run and repair the steam mechanism and the train was converted to diesel.

The tradition of the annual school picnics at Springbank Park began early in the century and continued for more than thirty years, dying out only when the streetcars stopped running to the park. On a day in June, all the public school children in the city travelled to the park by streetcar. The London Street Railway offered a special fare and added extra cars to accommodate the throngs. A program of sports and games worked up healthy appetites. "Parents are earnestly requested", read a 1929 picnic program, "to send an abundance of provisions, so that the little folks may have a genuine picnic." The Springbank picnic was the highlight of the school year, as this description suggests:

The day was one of the finest. The morning broke with every promise of ideal picnic weather, and juvenile hearts bounded with joy as they rolled out of bed and dressed with all the alacrity that stamps the picnic morning as against the day when school studies once more stare young hopefuls in the face . . .

At 12 o'clock the last train load of shouting and singing merrymakers from the schools left the city. The trolley sped away for the river park with its jolly load, and seemed to imbibe of the spirit of the occasion, inanimate thing though it looked.

To the mind of the London boy and girl, patriotic to the core, there is no park in all Christendom to match the river

Jimmie and Minnie Kennedy with the miniature steam train at Springbank Park, on the occasion of his retirement, July 30, 1965.

Strolling the riverbank at Springbank, c. 1920. Courtesy, Don Whetstone.

park. There is no spot to him where freedom and beauty so abound. Here he is, in the country, beside the sleepy river, and running about in the woods, and watching the rippling springs, and enjoying lunch and playing baseball and swinging in the swings and doing all manner of things at one and at the same time, and seeming not to know which to do first. (**London Free Press**, *June 16, 1905*)

In 1935, the Jones family leased the land of the municipal campground, which was no longer well used, from the Public Utilities Commission and built Wonderland Gardens, an outdoor dance hall and swimming pool. Later, an enclosed dance floor was added. (The Jones also owned the "Winter Gardens", a dance hall on Queens Avenue where Guy Lombardo played his first regular gig.) Wonderland Gardens is still a popular dance hall. The original outdoor bandstand is preserved, with mementoes of some of the famous bands who played there, including Glenn Miller, Lionel Thornton, Woody Herman, Count Basie and Guy Lombardo.

Storybook Gardens, a children's attraction envisioned by two Commission members, Earl Nichols and Elmo Curtis, after seeing a similar attraction in California, opened in June 1958 with one of the best unplanned publicity stunts ever. Just before the official opening, two sea lions were flown in from California. One of them, later dubbed "Slippery" in honour of his exploit, escaped into the Thames River. He swam down the Thames to Lake St. Clair, through the Detroit River, and into Lake Erie, before being captured near Sandusky, Ohio, by officials of the Toledo Zoo.

The story did not end with his re-capture. His captors claimed that, as he had been found in U.S. waters after the London P.U.C. had given up the search, they had the right to keep him. Londoners were outraged. Two P.U.C. Commissioners rushed off to Toledo, where officials soon relented. Slippery was made an honourary citizen and presented with the keys of the city, before being escorted home by zoo officials, together with Lucky, a baby puma, as a goodwill gift.

There is reason to suspect that the threat to keep Slippery in Toledo was merely a masterful public relations stunt. Years later Phil Skeldon, then director of the Toledo zoo and Slippery's captor, remarked: "I think we cooked that one up a little bit."

It worked. Slippery was given a tumultuous welcome on his return. Tens of thousands of Londoners lined the streets to watch his entourage pass, and many more poured into Storybook Gardens to admire the returning hero. The famous sea lion kept a low profile.

Slippery and Lonesome had their honeymoon haven in the Gardens today. Like any other newlyweds, they secluded themselves as far back in their enclosure as possible and just wouldn't budge for anything . . . "They spent a quiet night together," quipped Ted Foster, P.U.C. consultant, "They obviously had a lot to tell each other."
(**London Free Press**, *July 8, 1958*)

Since that time, Storybook Gardens has remained a favourite with London children and visitors. Slippery died in 1967, but is remembered by a life-size sculpture and map of his amazing odyssey.

It was not until the early 1960s that Reservoir Hill, part of the waterworks system from the outset, officially became a public park. Justly renowned for the

Slippery and his mate Lonesome, shortly after his return, July 1958.

view it affords of the Thames valley and the city, and for the magnificent stand of ancient trees preserved on its slopes, Reservoir Hill was, it is believed, the site of a skirmish during the War of 1812. According to one account, in October 1813 a British detachment being pursued by American soldiers after the Battle of Moraviantown took a stand on Reservoir, or as it was once called, Hungerford Hill. Mrs. McNames, a local pioneer, ''. . . sprang upon a baggage wagon and, regardless of the bullets which whistled around her, she handed out ammunition to the troops and carried water for them to drink during the whole of the engagement.''

During 1969, Reservoir Hill was again a battle ground. A piece of privately-owned land on the hill was sold to a developer, who announced plans for three 22-storey apartment buildings. Concerned citizens succeeded in stopping the development and preserving the hill in its natural state.

Another souvenir of the earliest history of Springbank is preserved in the small fieldstone structure known as ''Flint Cottage''. Robert Flint settled in the Byron area in 1836, and built a stone cottage for his family in 1837. When his son Pirney married, he built the second cottage, now used by the Garden Club, in 1857. The older cottage served as a station of the London Street Railway for many years.

Springbank Park is not the only park in London originally purchased as part of the municipal waterworks. By 1908, it had become apparent that Springbank could not provide enough water for the growing city. Several private interests proposed schemes to meet the shortfall. Finally, Adam Beck offered to drill a system of wells on the Parke and Gerry river flats near the corner of Ridout and Horton Streets, and supply the city with an additional million gallons of water a year. His proposal was put to the electorate in 1909. The **Free Press** vehemently opposed it, proposing, instead, the use of river water. Naturally, its arch rival, the **Advertiser**, supported Beck, even to the extent of publishing a picture of a dead cow lying on a riverbank. When the scheme was approved, Beck promised: ''We will retain the Parke and Gerry Flats for all time to come as parks and the children will have their playground forever.'' He kept his promise; the land became Thames Park.

Springbank Park is now linked to a series of other riverside parks and natural areas by bicycle and walking paths. Still London's premier park, it more than justifies James Egan's determination that Londoners should have a source of pure water.

"GREAT NEGLIGENCE": THE VICTORIA BOAT DISASTER.

Wm. D. Eckhart sworn: I am headmaster of London East Schools. On 24th I was on board of Victoria about 5 o'clock . . . I paid very little attention to the crowds who had got on until we had left the wharf. I was on the upper deck talking with Mr. Duffield when he called my attention and said the boat was not running right. A deck hand I believe named Starky was placed at the stairs to prevent people coming up or down . . . Some people were standing in about 10 inches of water and some with their boots off. I was finally persuaded that the hull was full of water as she seemed very tippish. When I came up again I saw a number who were greatly excited. I tried to pacify them from fear of a panic . . . Immediately after that the boat made a turn in the bend and the people in the stern moved slightly towards the centre but with no rush. Up to this time there was no panic. Immediately after this the boat went over or capsized. The boat almost completely turned over on its side so much so that it was impossible for anyone to keep on deck unless they had hold of something above them to support them. I was in the water with the rest . . .
(W. D. Eckhart's testimony to the Coroner's Inquest into death of Fanny Cooper, May 28th, 1881)

Mr. Eckhart was very lucky that he lived to tell his story — the story of the last trip of the steamer "Victoria".

It was a story that began in 1878, when London council bought land downriver at Coomb's Mill to build a municipal waterworks. Londoners soon discovered that the newly acquired public land was very picturesque — a perfect picnic spot, in fact. Access by road was almost impossible for most of the year, but Chestnut Park, as it was sometimes called, was a short and pleasant trip by boat from the forks. The waterworks dam kept the level of the Thames high enough to allow large vessels to operate on the route.

The first big steamer on the river was the "Forest City", launched in September 1878 by the Thames Navigation Company. During the 1879 season, a band was hired to play on board the "Forest City" and moonlight excursions were offered. A rival company, the London and Waterworks Line, launched the "Enterprise" in May, and the "Princess Louise" was added to the fleet of the Thames Navigation Company in June. By 1880, the hull of the "Enterprise", which had caught on fire during the winter, had been sold and re-built into a new ship, the ill-fated "Victoria".

Londoners were enthusiastic about steamer excursions. The boats were gay with fresh paint and wood trim. Some even boasted stained glass windows and other elegant fittings. There were many points of interest along the half-hour journey. Woodland Park was a favourite stop, as was the Anglican cemetery beside it. (Victorians treated cemeteries much like parks, as places to stroll and enjoy nature.) Ward's Hotel, famous for illegal gambling and other unsavoury activities, stood on the north bank, just opposite the waterworks. At Chestnut Park itself, there was a pavilion and other man-made attractions to add to those provided by nature.

Business was so good that a bitter rivalry grew up between the two boat companies, which led to several near accidents on the water. The worst of these incidents occurred on May 24, 1880. The "Forest City", owned by T.N.C. and the "Victoria", its competitor, were going downriver side by side. When passengers on the two steamers reached across to join hands, the captain of the "Forest City" decided that his boat was being grappled, and forced the "Victoria" into the riverbank.

Unfortunately, a large tree overhanging the steamer Victoria, raked the covering of the upper deck with its big branches, alarming the passengers who received yet a ruder shock when the vessel struck the shore . . . That however was not the end of it. When the Forest City was again returning to the Water Works, the delayed Victoria was just nearing the dredged channel and gave the signal for the Forest City to go to the left. Thus had marine laws been obeyed, it should have been answered and obeyed by the steamer, but it was not done in time . . . and a collision was the result . . .
(**London Free Press**, *May 25, 1880*)

Disaster was narrowly averted, and the passengers of the "Victoria" returned home with a tale to tell. A year later to the day, the "Victoria" was not so lucky.

May 24, 1881 was a beautiful spring day. Holidays were precious in the nineteenth century, and Londoners were determined to enjoy this one. Crowds descended on the docks at the forks to board the steamers bound for Chestnut Park.

By late afternoon, hundreds of tired picnickers waited on the Chestnut Park dock for the homeward journey. When the "Victoria" arrived, more than six hundred people swarmed aboard her. Her captain knew the boat was grossly overloaded. But no-one wanted to get off, and a crowd, especially a hot, tired one, is hard to shift.

It has never been clear what made the "Victoria" capsize, although it was believed that she tipped when the passengers rushed to one side to watch two racing skiffs go by. As she went over, the boiler came loose and crashed down, bringing the upper deck with it. At least 181 people were crushed or drowned. Most were children and women, weighed down by their heavy clothes.

Lambert Payne, a senior **Free Press** reporter, described what he saw when he arrived at the wreck later that night:

It was now dark, and two large bonfires were blazing

View of the Wreck of the Victoria, 1881.

Wreck of the Victoria, 1881. This photograph was obviously faked, probably by superimposing images of small boats and spectators on a picture of the accident site taken the following day.

The "Victoria" and the "Princess Louise" at the landing at the Forks, with the Sulphur Springs in the background, c.1880.

on the bank. These fires cast a weird light over the scene — a scene that will never be blotted from my mind while memory lasts. It was unreal. It took on the character of a nightmare. Scores of men were breaking up the two decks of the steamer, which lay like a blanket over the surface of the water. The drownings had all taken place within 30 or 40 feet of the shore — most of them within 15. The sister vessel, the "Princess Louise", was drawn up alongside, and to her deck the dead were being carried. I pulled myself together and began getting names.

At midnight the "Princess Louise" left the scene of the disaster with her cargo of dead, and 20 minutes later was at her dock. I made the count on the way up to the city, and there were 152 bodies. These were laid out on the lawn at the old Sulphur Springs bathhouse . . .

At four in the morning, without having thought of either food or sleep, I returned to the river. I joined in the search for bodies, and before 10 o'clock my pike pole had brought up more than a score. Two of them, I remember, were children of my associate at the "The Advertiser", Charlie Matthews . . .
(**London Free Press**, *May 25, 1881*)

A grief-stricken city buried its dead; hearses and funeral processions clogged the streets for days. A joint procession was held for Fanny Cooper, and her fiance, Willie Glass, who were to have been married in mid-June. Joseph Coughlin buried two daughters, a son and two grand-children as a result of the accident. George Evans lost his wife and four children. Few families were untouched.

The inquest was a long and involved process. The verdict damned everyone, including the Government:

We the Jury . . . do find that the capsizing of the Steamer Victoria was caused by water in the hold . . . We are also of the opinion that the engineer was guilty of great negligence in the discharge of his duty in not seeing that the hold was clear of water and in not conveying in person to the captain the dangerous condition of the boat. We think that the captain was to blame in accepting the dual position of captain and wheelsman which prevented him from giving his undivided attention to the proper management of the boat . . . The jury thinks that the Government Inspector deserves blame for the manner in which he inspected and passed the boat Victoria last year . . . and we would strongly urge upon the Government the necessity of enabling more stringent inspections and regulations in regard to passenger steam boats.
(Coroner's Inquest into the death of Fanny Cooper, May 1881)

The captain and the business manager of the line were arrested, but later released and acquitted of all charges.

Boating on the Thames slowed to a trickle. By July, the "Forest City" and the "Princess Louise" were up for sale. Two large and melancholy engravings, as well as postcards, stereoscope views, poems and other souvenirs of the terrible tragedy became popular items. Steamboat cruises throughout Eastern Canada lost money. Port Stanley became the preferred holiday spot for Londoners. A **Free Press** editor, writing in 1886, observed: "Thousands used to visit Chestnut Park, but since the accident, it has lapsed into its old obscurity."

In the early summer of 1883, the "Princess Louise", which had not been sold, was refurbished and began to operate again. That July, the Thames flooded. The "Princess" was torn from her moorings and carried down the river to be smashed against the Byron bridge. The "Forest City" survived the storm and was later dismantled.

In 1888, two new boats were built to make the trip from the forks to Springbank. By then, the Pipeline road had been improved and there was competition from a horse-drawn bus service. Business dwindled away when the London Street Railway opened its line to the park in 1896, and by 1898, the steamer service was discontinued. London's steamboat days were over.

The Forks of the Thames, with the steamer Forest City at landing, c. 1880.

"ALL THE TIME RISING": FLOODS IN LONDON.

October 18, 1795 — Michael preached, and as it has been rainy the whole week, so that the river was unusually high, and the corn of several brethren under water, they helped one another to save it, whereby all were busy who were able, and so they continued to do the next day, for the water was all the time rising.
(Diary of David Zeisberger, Moravian missionary, near Thamesville, Ontario, 1795)

For as long as records are available, the Thames has overflowed its banks. And the people who live along it have worked together to undo the damage.

In the early years, as David Zeisberger's diary suggests, Thames valley pioneers accepted the fact that the river burst its banks from time to time. They were careful to build their homes a safe distance from the water. The silt deposited by flooding was considered a boon to agriculture, and logs and rafts of lumber could be floated downstream on the crest of spring freshets. Settlers were more concerned if, after several dry, mild years, the river shrank and could no longer power the mills.

But as time went on, flooding became a more serious problem. Deforestation and ice jams caused by the increasing number of mill dams and bridges made floods more dangerous. The flimsy wooden bridges which connected London to the south and west were quickly swept away when the river rose. As the town grew, houses were built on the river flats, so that flooding threatened not only fields and bridges, but also people.

The flood of 1846 was remembered as especially severe. Nearly forty years later, one man recalled:

. . . the loss was very heavy to the farmers all along the Thames. Hundreds of horses, cattle and swine were swept down the river, the banks near the city being literally covered with dead bodies. A great many people lost everything they had. Rich men were suddenly made poor.
(**London Advertiser**, July 11, 1883)

During the 1860s, four floods caused widespread damage in the London area, the worst occurring in the spring of 1868. In 1873, parts of the suburb of Kensington (West London) were under ten feet of water for two days, and the following January, conditions were even worse. Two lives were lost in 1874.

But it was in July, 1883 that the Thames rose to its full fury.

On the night of July 10, during a severe thunderstorm, a bolt of lightning struck an oil refinery in London East, causing a spectacular fire. A reporter, returning from the fire, stopped to look at the river and saw a wall of water moving towards London West. Disaster followed swiftly.

The uninterrupted torrents of rain which fell all last night swelled the river to a height altogether unknown at this sea-

SAD DETAILS.

London West's Deplorable Visitation.

20 Victims Engulphed by the Waters.

Anxious Enquiry for Many Reported Missing.

Touching Scenes and Pathetic Incidents of the Flood.

Heavy Loss and Suspension of Traffic on the Railways.

Houses Dashed to Pieces and Bridges Swept Away.

Headlines, *London Advertiser*, July 12, 1883.

son of the year. At 2 o'clock a.m., it was as high as at the great spring freshet, and was filled with timber and driftwood that threatened to carry away Kensington bridge. A large part of London West was flooded, and men, women and children fled from their homes to the city. The water was rising rapidly in the houses . . .
(**London Advertiser**, *July 11, 1883*)

By morning, the scene from Blackfriar's Bridge, one of the few bridges to survive the night, was frighteningly unfamiliar:

Standing upon the bluff on the city side of the river, a vast sea was presented to the view. Here and there the tops of houses appeared, while outhouses in all distorted shapes and positions, with fencing, cordwood, lumber and all the floatable debris, eddied and whirled about. Standing on the precarious foothold afforded by a wood pile, a man in dishabille was wildly crying for someone to go to his rescue.
(**London Advertiser**, *July 11, 1883*)

A valiant effort by rescuers saved the man on the woodpile, but many were not as lucky. The strength of the current, combined with the large amount of floating debris, made tragedy inevitable. One man later recalled:

Among the first things I saw was a spectacle that wrung my heart. A family had decided to take refuge in a tree which grew close to their front door. The mother and several of the children had been transferred in safety. Last of all the baby was being passed up, when suddenly, the house was torn from its foundations and dashed against the tree. The baby was caught between the tree and the house and was crushed to death. The shape of its little body was plainly marked on the house in crimson.
(**London Free Press**, *July 12, 1883*)

In all, eighteen people died as a result of the flood. Many houses were swept away and never recovered, and four hundred of those which remained were made uninhabitable.

The river flooded on the south branch some hours after it inundated London West. By then the fire bells had been ringing for some time and the inhabitants were able to reach high ground without loss of life. When the force of the flood began to abate, the heartbreaking tasks of repairing the damage began.

Considering their troubles the villagers bore up bravely, and cheered by the spontaneous assistance from the city and vicinity took heart again. In all directions the work of preserving household goods and restoring homes was seen in active progress. Today another bountiful supply of food and clothing will be sent from the city, and the villagers will enjoy the luxury of pure water from the city mains.
(**London Advertiser**, *July 12, 1883*)

Londoners learned nothing from the flood of 1883. Houses were rebuilt on the river flats. A flimsy dike constructed in West London collapsed under the force of water in March, 1898. It was rebuilt, but proved inadequate again only six years later.

At 1:00 a.m. on March 26, 1904, a horseman galloped through London West shouting that the water had risen over the top of the rebuilt dike, and the evacuation began. Bad weather conditions added to the terror of those forced to flee their homes:

During the early morning there was a decided change in the temperature prevailing. The mercury quickly dropped below the freezing point and strong winds blew from the north. While people were boat load after boat load being brought from their place of residence to higher ground at the west end of the Kensington Bridge, flurries of snow fell and the scene was a very wintry one. Many of the people were scantily clad in the hurry with which they had left...
(**London Free Press**, *March 28, 1904*)

Arthur J. Clark was one of the many volunteers who helped rescue the stranded residents of London West. He escaped from his Walnut Street home with his wife and children at 5 a.m. Once his family was safe on high ground, he returned to the flood scene:

Then I got a boat . . . I was busy taking people out of their homes. I think that I took out forty children alone . . . One old lady I went after on Mount Pleasant Avenue would not leave her house until I had caught her chickens and put them in the pantry.
(**London Free Press**, *March 29, 1904*)

In 1905, the dikes were rebuilt and extended, but in 1918, 1929, 1935 and 1936 flooding caused considerable damage to the unprotected flats in North and South London.

The flood of 1937 was the worst ever recorded on the Thames.

Heavy rainfalls during the week of April 21 to 27 produced nearly six inches of rain in London. The ground was already saturated from the spring thaw and earlier rains, and could absorb no more. In the early hours of April 26, the North Branch rose at Fanshawe. Broughdale and part of North London were quickly flooded, and the water soon reached to top of the West London dikes. Flooding on the South Branch was also severe. At the high water mark, over five hundred acres of London lay under water.

Many years later, one woman whose family lived near the Wellington Street Bridge, recalled the day of the flood:

Coming home from school, the first thing I saw was the water almost to the top of the bridge and everything floating in the river — furniture, chairs, sheds. It was chaos at home and they put me to work trying to get everything we could upstairs. The people down on Front Street got flooded every spring — but never like this — so they were all bringing their stuff up to our place . . . One house from Front Street just lifted off its foundation and the whole thing went floating away. Mrs. Loveday lived down there with seven children and when the flood moved through it seemed to take everything, including her baby's crib . . . We lost our home and our livelihood . . .
(Betty Galarneau, in **London Magazine***, April, 1987)*

Once again, volunteers worked through the night to take flood victims off by boat. Joseph L. Britton, the only fatality of the '37 flood, was drowned when the rowboat he was using was swamped.

Sketches of flood damage, July 1883, executed by Paul Peel for publication in the *London Free Press*.

Flood damage in South London, probably March 1904.

The level of the river had begun to drop by 7 a.m. on April 27, and by noon, had fallen dramatically. London's water supply was cut by half owing to damage to pipes and pumping stations. Fire posed a serious threat. A banner in heavy black print on the front page of the **Free Press** advised: "Boil all the water you drink; take no chances with typhoid." Health authorities innoculated many flood victims against typhoid.

By the morning of the 28th, the city was bathed in bright spring sunshine. The clean-up began.

As dusk fell last night, hundreds of weary, discouraged men and women, their clothes splattered with mud and their feet soaking wet, trooped out of West London. It was a sad looking army of flood workers who had worked all day . . . trying to reclaim all they could from the ravaged area . . . When darkness fell West London was a ghost town. It was a strange sight . . . Out on front lawns were piled pianos, chesterfields, bedroom suites and kitchen stoves. Doors stood open, verandahs tilted crazily, and garages were piled in strange places.
(**London Free Press**, *April 29, 1937*)

The streets of Broughdale, the first of the affected areas to be passable, were crowded with the cars of sightseers, curious to see the damage for themselves. There was plenty to see: private and public losses in London were estimated at $900,000.

The lesson of the '37 flood was very clear. According to Dr. J.D. Detwiler, a professor of biology at Western: ". . . By a system of well-placed dams, we should reclaim for the rivers and streams some of their original heritage — their excess water storage basins." (**London Free Press**, *April 27, 1937*). West London residents pressed the city to take action, and even threatened to hold a tax strike if nothing was done. The city turned to the provincial government for assistance, but war intervened.

The 1947 flood was almost as severe as that of 1937 in some places on the river. West London was lucky:

Flood damage, looking northwest from Dundas St. Bridge, 1947. In '47, the water reached the top of the dike at high water point.

it was evacuated and the dikes were reinforced with sandbags, but damage was minimal. On the south branch, 150 houses and some factories were flooded. The city engineer, W. M. Veitch, in his report on the flood, wrote:

The recommendation made by me in 1938 is again submitted, namely that the proper protection of London West can only be attained by the construction of a dam, or dams, on the North Branch of the River Thames, at Fanshawe or elsewhere above that point.

(**London Free Press**, *April 9, 1947*)

In August 1947, the Upper Thames River Conservation Authority was formed, with the co-operation of all municipalities up river from London. A reforestation program began at once. Ground was broken for the Fanshawe Dam in 1950, and it was completed in 1952.

Necessity was once again the mother of a London park. The four mile-long lake formed by the dam was developed into a swimming and sailing facility, and Fanshawe Park, complete with beaches and campgrounds, took shape.

In 1956, the Authority endorsed a proposal for a Pioneer Village at the park. With the assistance of London archaeologist Wilfrid Jury, pioneer buildings were reconstructed or moved to the site and filled with authentic artifacts, many on permanent loan from Dr. Jury himself.

It is appropriate that among the buildings at Fanshawe Pioneer Village is the homestead of the painter Paul Peel, one of London's most famous sons. Although Peel spent most of his professional career in Paris, before leaving London he did several illustrations for publication in the London Free Press. The subject of the drawings — the flood of 1883.

Flood Damage at Labatt Park, April, 1937.

"COOL, HEALTH-GIVING BREEZES": LONDON'S LAKESIDE PARK

The park and grounds at Port Stanley, long an eye-sore to the citizens of London, when taken over by the Commission were found in a condition of extreme neglect . . . Under such circumstances it was decided that it would be good policy to spend whatever money was necessary to make Port Stanley as attractive as possible. The cost, it was felt, would be justified by the increased business which would come to the railway . . .
(**London Railway Commission Annual Report**, *1919*)

Londoners of 1919 considered Port Stanley their own private lakeside park. And indeed, much of the beach and parkland did belong to the city, through its ownership of the London and Port Stanley Railway. It was the L. and P.S. which linked the fortunes of the two towns for over a hundred years.

The railway was built in the 1850s by a group of prominent London businessmen, backed by local municipal and county governments. The city of London invested heavily, for the L. and P.S. was to be an important link between land-bound London and the Great Lakes. The railway never developed a profitable freight business, but Londoners soon began to take advantage of easy access to the pretty town of Port Stanley. It was the site of London's second annual civic picnic in 1857. After Confederation Day, July 1, 1867, the **Free Press** reported:

Port Stanley was the great attraction point on Monday, not less than 4,000 persons having visited that place during the day. The picnic grounds were covered with human beings, and the lake was liberally patronized with bathers, hundreds embracing the luxury of a good wash and a swim. Others danced in the large shed built on the grounds, while some employed their time in swings, cricket and other diversions.
(**London Free Press**, *July 2, 1867*)

In 1871, the Fraser House, a large and commodious hotel, was built on Invererie Heights overlooking the lake, and soon became a popular resort for wealthy Londoners. An incline railway was built from the beach to the Heights. It was powered by a used Great Western Railway steam locomotive, which also produced enough steam to run a merry-go-round. The incline railway, later converted to electricity, ran until the early 1960s, when a government inspector required prohibitively expensive repairs.

The first summer home in Port Stanley was built

Port Stanley, c. 1925

Incline Railway at Port Stanley, c. 1925.

in 1883 by two brothers. They were both ministers, one from London and one from St. Thomas. An unusual feature of their cottage was the moveable front wall, which could be raised to provide shelter for outdoor activities. In 1887, a **Free Press** editorial wondered why others did not follow the example of the two clergymen.

In this broiling heat, they are well off who are in summer cottages by the lakeside. A few of these are to be found at Port Stanley, but why are there not more?
(**London Free Press**, *July, 1887*)

And soon, of course, there were more. By 1944, cottagers, many of them Londoners, swelled the summertime population of Port Stanley by 5,000.

For day-trippers, picnicking on Invererie Heights continued to be the most popular attraction. A turn-of-the century newspaper reported:

Hardly a day passes during the season but excursionists from some part of Western Ontario find their way to these heights where beneath the broad spreading trees, the tablecloths are laid, and justice done to the ample provisions brought by the ladies from their homes. Cold and hot water are provided on the grounds and for the children there is plenty of amusement on the merry-go-rounds and swings.
(**London Free Press**, *May 24, 1900*)

Popular as Port Stanley was, passenger business alone was not enough to make the L. and P.S. profitable. It was leased to the Great Western Railway from 1872 to 1892, and then to the Lake Erie and Detroit River Railway (later the Pere Marquette Railway), until 1913. When the lease with the Pere Marquette expired, Sir Adam Beck persuaded the City of London, which had, by default, become the majority shareholder, to electrify the line. The L. and P.S. was to become a prototype of the province-wide electric rail system he envisioned for the future.

The Railway owned extensive lands in Port Stanley, both on the beach and on Invererie Heights. Beck realized that, in order to justify the expenditure to electrify the railway, Londoners would have to be enticed to visit Port Stanley in greater numbers. He began to improve and add to the facilities.

The incline railway was bought from private interests and the grounds at the foot of the hill were levelled and landscaped. Then in 1916, a combined bathhouse and cafeteria was constructed on the beach.

The interior of the Cafeteria is decorated in buff with wood trimmings, and presents a clean and attractive appearance. The atmosphere is wholesome, the place is well lighted, and excellent ventilation is insured through large

Picnic Hill at Port Stanley, c. 1930.

screen windows the whole width of the south side overlooking the lake . . . The Bath House occupies the greater portion of the building . . . The west end is devoted to the men's compartment, and the east to that of the women patrons. Each end is equipped with 50 private dressing rooms . . . while there are also 322 steel lockers. The Bath House is equipped with a complete sanitary laundry capable of sterilizing, washing and drying hundreds of suits an hour.
(**London Railways Commission Annual Report**, *1918*)

Perhaps it was the influence of Beck which ensured that the Bath House even offered electric hair dryers free of charge for the use of its lady patrons.

Other improvements followed. An old dance pavilion on the Heights was made into the Japanese Tea House, decorated with paper umbrellas and chinese lanterns. Swings, drinking fountains, maypoles and washrooms were added for the picnickers.

As more Londoners were attracted to Port Stanley, concessions began to line the beach boardwalk. Mackie's, which served a special orangeade created by its owner ("Often Imitated, Never Duplicated"), opened in 1911. The Erie Amusement Company opened a roller coaster on the beach, and soon ice cream stalls, hamburger and fruit stands, a photography studio, a bowling alley, an open-air theatre and other attractions were added. A 1923 promotional brochure called Port Stanley the "Coney Island of Western Ontario."

At one end of the boardwalk stood the privately-owned Casino, which opened in 1909. There was a dance hall on the second floor, picnic tables on the first, and outside, a ferris wheel and excursion boats. In 1926, the London Railway Commission built a second dance hall at the other end of the boardwalk.

Dance lovers, young and old, thronged to Port Stanley last night to attend the opening of the new dance pavilion of the L. and P.S. Railway, and dance for the first time on one of Canada's finest dance floors . . . The place as a whole is so utterly and fascinatingly strange to the familiar dance halls that no words can describe it. The floor is placed well above the level of the earth, giving free access to the breeze . . . Huge lanterns of fantastic shapes and colourings diffuse a soft glow throughout the great room . . . Four spotlights in the four corners of the room throw beams of different colours on a huge revolving globe made up of tiny vari-shaped crystals. The crystals fill the room with darting beams of coloured lights.
(**London Free Press**, *July 30, 1926*)

The Famous Vincent Lopez band from New York played for the crowd of 6,000 which attended the opening. The Pavilion, later re-named the Stork Club, continued to be popular until the 1970s. It closed in 1973, but was refurbished and re-opened in 1974 by London businessman and Port Stanley resident Joe McManus Jr. In 1979, a serious fire damaged the building beyond repair.

The annual Scotch and Irish picnics, a Port Stanley tradition since before the turn of the century, featured baby contests, races, music and dance competitions, baseball games and many other events. In 1923, the Irish picnic coincided with the London Old Boy's Reunion, making it an even more elaborate event than usual:

No stone had been left unturned in an effort to make the day a crowning success and there was something hap-

The Bathhouse at Port Stanley, c. 1925.

The Vincent Lopez Band posing in the newly opened London and Port Stanley Pavilion, 1929.
They are arranged on the landing between the first and second floor;
the dance floor may be glimpsed in the upper right corner of the picture.

pening every moment from the arrival of the first visitors early in the morning till the departure of the last tired but happy merrymaker near the midnight hour. There were baby shows that brought record entries, races for the boys and girls, contests for the older men and women, as well as the usual fat men's race, oldest member on the grounds and all the other picnic features that go toward making an outing of this kind a success. Then there were daylight fireworks and concerts, a swim in good old Lake Erie's waters and last but not by any means least, there were the invigorating, cool, health-giving breezes . . .
(**London Free Press**, *August 10, 1923*)

Many London companies treated their employees to an annual picnic at Port Stanley. The companies paid the train fares, and supplied the food, games and prizes. A typical company picnic was described in 1943:

The third annual picnic of the Hobbs Glass Welfare Association was held at Port Stanley on Thursday. A crowd of some 400 employees, their families and friends travelled to the lakeside resort to enjoy the outing. During the afternoon, a variety program of sports and games were enjoyed. Ice cream and soft drinks were served. A lively game of baseball was enjoyed in the evening . . . The highlight of the day was the fine chicken supper which was prepared and served by the Women's Guild of Epiphany Church.
(**London Free Press**, *August 3, 1943*)

The London and Port Stanley Railway was in financial difficulty again by the mid-1930s. It was transferred from the Railway Commission to the Public Utilities Commission in 1936 and some economies were introduced. With the added traffic of servicemen stationed in and around London, the railway and Port Stanley experienced a brief boom during the war years. An advertisement for the opening of the 1944 season read:

With the 24th of May the season of holiday and happiness really starts at Port Stanley. The fun and merriment will start off with a big bang in the personal appearance Thursday of Harold Austin and his great American orchestra . . . Joe Broderick, manager of the Port Stanley pavilion, confidently predicts that this will be Port's biggest and most successful season.
(*Advertisement in* **London Free Press**, *May 22, 1944*)

Mr. Broderick's optimism was justified. Over a million people travelled the railway each year from 1942 until 1946, with a high in 1943 of 1,705,233.

When gas rationing was lifted, traffic on the railway dropped off and continued to decline throughout the 50s. Passenger service was ended in 1957 and in 1966, the line was traded to the Canadian National Railways in exchange for several pieces of industrial property.

The days of Port Stanley as London's own private lakeside park were over, although for many Londoners, the memories are still bright.

The boardwalk at Port Stanley, c. 1925.

Playing in the surf at Port Stanley, c. 1925.

LONDON'S PARKS UNDER E.V. BUCHANAN

I am a Scottish Calvinist — If I do something well, I can't take credit because it was fore-ordained. And if I do something wrong, I can't be blamed. So it is a good philosophy.
(**London Free Press**, *May 28, 1983*)

E.V. Buchanan did many things well, not the least of which was managing London's parks for almost forty years. In his long term as manager of the P.U.C., the parks system reached full maturity.

Buchanan's father was a bookseller in Hamilton, Scotland. Edward Victor trained as an engineer at the Technical College, Glasgow. Shortly after graduating, he read about the Niagara hydro-electric project and decided to emigrate to Canada. He arrived in Toronto in 1910 and found temporary work with the fledgling Hydro Commission. After a meeting with Adam Beck, London's apostle of hydro-electricity, Buchanan was offered the job of resident engineer on the city substation.

The meeting with Beck was the beginning of a long personal and working relationship. Buchanan later remembered:

. . . Walking home one evening with one of London's prominent citizens whom I had just met, he left me by saying "Good night, I'm glad to have met you but sorry you are involved with that crook Beck." This was the beginning of my realization that Adam Beck was a highly controversial figure . . . It was only a few days later that Beck visited the job. He approached me brusquely and demanded to know who I was and all about me. He ended his conversation by saying "Well I suppose Scotland is a good place to come from!"
(**The History of London's Water Supply**, *E.V. Buchanan*)

In 1911, Buchanan became the Chief Electrical Engineer to the London Board of Water Commissioners, under H.J. Glaubitz, the General Manager.

Until 1912, the city's parks were controlled by two different bodies, the Parks Committee of city council and the Board of Water Commissioners. In 1912, Council created a Board of Park Management and placed it under the Water Commissioners. According to Parks Commissioner and noted naturalist W.E. Saunders, parks were important economically, as well as aesthetically:

If the city be kept in nice condition, so that people who come here will admire it, they will want to come here to live, and will advertise us, and we will get the manufacturers as well . . . A city can afford to spend money on beautifying itself.
(**London Free Press**, *November 10, 1912*)

In 1914, the Board of Water Commissioners was re-named the Public Utilities Commission.

Soon after the outbreak of war, Buchanan's superior, Glaubitz, an unpopular German immigrant, came under suspicion.

One of the first charges brought against him arose from the case of a young German lad working in the Engineering Department. On the evening of the declaration of war Glaubitz told his young compatriot that he should get out of the country quickly. This, the lad decided to do, but wanted his pay before he left. Glaubitz then asked A.O. Hunt, the Assistant Manager, to give the lad his pay and take an I.O.U. for the amount. Thus Glaubitz came to be accused of aiding and abetting the escape of an enemy.
(**Roses in December**, *E.V. Buchanan*)

Glaubitz was suspended, and then re-instated on the condition that he resign. Buchanan's appointment as his replacement was the one good thing to come out of this unsavoury incident.

Buchanan soon became an active supporter of the campaign for public playgrounds.

A sound body is the first requisite of good citizenship. The benefits accruing from playgrounds must be apparent to all thoughtful citizens, and that only the children of the well-to-do with their country homes should have good air and sunlight in which to exercise and grow, presupposes a continuance of the narrow view of community prosperity.
(**P.U.C. Annual Report**, *1918*)

In 1920 a playground program was established under the aegis of the P.U.C. Buchanan freely admitted that his training as an engineer did not prepare him for his new responsibilities.

I tried to learn all I could about parks and recreation. I visited parks, zoos and playgrounds in many places in Canada, the U.S. and Europe. I have found that only good came of admitting one's ignorance of a subject and that people were flattered to be consulted and became most helpful.
(**Roses in December**)

Buchanan continued throughout his long career to take a keen interest in recreation. One of his proudest accomplishments was the creation of a public golf course. After a trip to Britain in 1922, during which he visited several municipal courses, he suggested that the Commission develop a course on public land across the river from Springbank Park.

The Chairman of the Commission Jared Vining, a prominent lawyer, objected that the Commission had no statutory right to own and operate a golf course. I asked if the golf course did not cost the taxpayer any money, who would object? He asked, how can you do it without any money? I said that I might be able to raise the money and had estimated that I could build one hole and green for $1,000 so that we might start with six holes or a total of $6,000. At that time, I was a member of the Rotary Club and offered the members one year's membership in the Municipal golf course for $10, promising to return the money if the golf course was not built.
(**Roses in December**)

Between the Rotarians and London's school teachers, Buchanan was able to raise $5,500 in membership fees for his non-existent course. The last $500 was

Water Commissioners, City Council and Officials at Springbank, May 1, 1911. The occasion was the switching on of hydro electric power to operate the water pumps at the Springbank pumphouse. Fron Row, from left to right: Ald. Bill Wilson; Ald. Burleigh Bennett; Ald. Bill Saunders; Commissioner Tom W. Mcfarland; not known; Commissioner Philip Pocock; Mayor Beattie; Commissioner Marr; Hon. Adam Beck; Engineer H. J. Glaubitz; Robert Greene; Engineer E.V. Buchanan; Editor of the London Echo.

a donation from Ralph Conable, General Manager of Woolworths in Canada, who was involved in a similar project in Toronto.

He walked over the land with me and said that this was an excellent place for a golf course and to go ahead. I told him that I had only $5,500 and that I promised the Commission I would not start until I had obtained $6,000. He asked for a blank cheque and immediately wrote one out for $500.

(Roses in December)

The first six holes opened in June, and another three were added before the end of the year. Buchanan played the first round, cheered by a large contingent of fans.

Buchanan had a cable stretched across the river and a flat-bottomed boat built, so that golfers who travelled out by the Springbank streetcar could pull themselves across to the course. Later, a suspension bridge was built.

By 1926, there were eighteen holes. The **London Free Press** commented:

Perhaps the outstanding accomplishment of the London Public Utilities Commission in recent years has been the establishment of the Thames Valley golf course . . . Here the average citizen can secure all the beneficial exercise which always attends participation in the game of golf, and he can also assimilate that peace of mind that is a natural result of being out in the open where blue skies, fresh green growing things and the songs of carefree birds all combine to make him feel that it's a pretty good old world after all.

(London Free Press, *May 29, 1926)*

Eventually another nine holes were added and a second public course was established at Fanshawe Park. According to Buchanan: "It never cost the taxpayer a penny."

During Buchanan's term as Manager of the P.U.C., many new parks came into being. One of the first was Basil Grover Park. In 1915, when it became clear that the city needed to increase the water supply, a group of businessmen offered to sell the city 4 acres of land with wells near the corner of Commissioners and Wharncliffe Road for $40,000. Buchanan, who thought the price exorbitant, was able to buy an adjacent 14 acre piece of land, which became Grover Park, for only $10,000. But not without making enemies:

One member of the group came to my office and said that his friends were most influential and that as City Council was considering the appointment of a City Manager they could ensure that I got the job. Of course in return I was to recommend the purchase of their property at their price. When I said "No" the reply was that there would be a utilities manager out of a job.
(Roses in December)

E.V. Buchanan worked hard to promote public interest in parks, speaking and writing about them at every opportunity. In 1934 he wrote:

The people of our cities are too apt in these days to think only of civic affairs as matters of book-keeping and engineering instead of realising the importance of making our cities beautiful places in which to live and bring up children who are the future citizens.
(The Echo, *March 22, 1934)*

His efforts to make Londoners more aware of "the importance of making our cities beautiful places" were successful. The parks system benefited by many generous donations.

Colonel William Moir Gartshore donated Chelsea Green Park to the city in 1915. Gartshore was general manager of McClary's Stove Works, a director of Canada Trust, and a colonel in the militia. He was also London's shortest-lived mayor. Gartshore was elected by a small margin in 1916. His opponent demanded a recount, which resulted in a tie. The City Clerk cast the deciding vote against Gartshore, who stepped down after only 16 days in office.

What is now Gibbons Park was orginally Becher's Island, owned by the Bechers of "Thornwood", the elegant mansion which overlooks it from St. George Street. Originally surrounded by the river on the north and east, and a mill stream on the south and west, the Island had long been a popular picnic spot. Describing activities on Dominion Day, 1867, the **Free Press** reported:

Others joined in parties and had a good time of it on Becher's Island, or singly in fishing, bathing or in accordance with their tastes.
(London Free Press, *July 2, 1867)*

In 1926, Mrs. Ronald Harris asked Buchanan to buy the land on behalf of her family for a park in honour of her father, Sir George Gibbons, a respected barrister and member of the International Waterways

Scene at the first tee, Thames Valley Golf Course, 1933. The four players were 'greats' of their time: from left to right, Joe Kirkwood, Sandy Somerville, Gene Sarazen, Jack Nash. Courtesy, Thames Valley Golf Club.

Commission. Buchanan agreed readily and assured her that the swampy land could be purchased cheaply. But that was not what Mrs. Harris wanted.

She said that old Mrs. Becher was not in good financial circumstances and that through this transaction good could be done in two ways. I was to go and offer to buy the property on the Gibbons family's behalf for not less than $25,000. Mrs. Becher was not to be told that the Gibbons were buying the land, only that I was buying on behalf of the City. It was a delicate business getting the price up to $25,000 but I believed I handled the deal with some finesse.
(Roses in December)

The land was cleared of trees and bush during the Depression by two teams of 50 men working with shovels and wheelbarrows.

The Gibbons family continued to take an active interest in the lovely park created on Becher's Island, and made several gifts towards its development. With some gentle persuasion from Buchanan, Miss Helen Gibbons, Mrs. Harris' sister, donated $20,000 to build a pool at the park in 1950.

When I reported my success at the next Board meeting, Commissioner Lewis said ''We should congratulate the Manager'' but Mayor Wenige, who did not like me, said it was Miss Gibbons who was giving the pool and not Buchanan. The Chairman Bev Hay said ''All right, let's thank Miss Gibbons and congratulate the Manager.''
(Roses in December)

Another donation to the parks system during Buchanan's time was Windermere, the home of Elsie Perrin Williams, heiress of the Perrin Biscuit Company fortune. Mrs. Williams' will gave her housekeeper, Harriet Corbett, a life interest in her large estate, provided that she care for Mrs. Williams' dog, Shaker. On Miss Corbett's death, the estate was to revert to the City of London. The city broke the will and settled with some of Mrs. Williams' outraged relatives in 1938. The city's share of the money was used to build the Elsie Perrin Williams Memorial Library and a wing of Victoria Hospital. Miss Corbett remained in solitary possession of house and grounds until her death in 1979. Windermere has since become a convention centre (operated by the Heritage London Foundation) and park. Its former owners, Elsie Perrin Williams and her husband, Dr. Hadley T. Williams, are buried on the grounds, surrounded by the graves of their beloved dogs.

In 1948, a house on Dundas Street near Colborne was donated by the daughter of Dr. J.B. Campbell. The house had once belonged to William Saunders, Director of the first Federal Experimental Farms, and was the boyhood home of Sir Charles Saunders, who developed the Marquis wheat strain, W.E. Saunders, a noted naturalist, and three other brothers. The house was demolished and a formal garden, with a fountain and reflecting pool, created on the property.

Swimming Camp at Gibbon's Park, 1929. Note the bathhouse at far right.

The grounds of 'Windermere', the Perrin country estate, c. 1900, with a rustic log bridge in the foreground. The estate was given to Elsie Perrin and her husband Dr. Hadley Williams as a wedding gift, and bequeathed to the city by Mrs. Williams. It is now a park and convention centre. Courtesy, Heritage London.

Amongst other notable donations were: Rowntree Playground, donated by Chester Rowntree, former president of Lawson and Jones and member of the first playgrounds advisory board; Belvedere Park, the last fragment of the once grand mansion "Belvedere", built by William Simpson Smith in 1875, donated by his heirs when the estate was subdivided in 1925; Silverwood Park, the gift of A.E. Silverwood, whose small egg and poultry buying depot which opened in London in 1903 grew into the mammoth Silverwood Dairies; Meredith Playground, donated by the distinguished family of lawyers and bankers; McMahen; and Doidge Park, a former gravel pit developed through the efforts of the North London Kiwanis Club. Doidge Park is only one of many contributions by local service clubs. Kiwanis Park, a 200 acre green belt along Pottersburg Creek, began with a purchase of land by the London Kiwanis Club in 1949.

Buchanan continued to campaign for parks long after he had retired from the P.U.C. During the 1950s, he was involved in the creation of the Pinery Provincial Park and served on the City Planning Board. His arguments for open space had the same pragmatic tone as those of William Saunders in 1912.

Open space pays for itself. If we are to attract more industry we should realize that modern industrialists make intensive studies of all the factors for a good location and probably the most important one is a healthy, happy and intelligent labor force. Open spaces contribute to this healthy body and mind.
(London Free Press, *December 20, 1969)*

He became involved in the debate over the forks of the Thames during the 1970s, opposing the construction of a modern art gallery on a piece of desirable parkland. When shown a drawing of the proposed gallery, he likened it to ". . . a collection of oil storage tanks."

Late in life, Buchanan wrote:
I think that my association with parks and recreation changed to a great extent my outlook on life. My education and training and work had been in the physical sciences and engineering and dealing only with inanimate things, but now I became involved in human affairs, the living environment and social endeavours.
(Roses in December)

Buchanan's professional involvements went far beyond parks and recreation. Among many other contributions to London, he promoted the early use of electricity, managed the London and Port Stanley Railway, helped found the faculty of Engineering at Western, and was involved in the development of University Hospital. He also wrote histories of electricity and water supply in London, and his autobiography, **Roses in December**. In reference to his book on the water supply, he once said wryly: "It's priceless. I know it's priceless because it couldn't sell a copy."

When E.V. Buchanan died in 1987, Dr. Edward Pleva, noted geographer, said: "He represented the last of London's youth and adolescence. This town is filled with a great number of firsts that orignated in his mind."

Saunders Pond, 1916. W.E. Saunders and his brother Charles are launching the canoe.

"THE PROPER SPIRIT OF PLAY": SPORTS AND RECREATION IN LONDON PARKS

It was one of the all-time great baseball stories. The scene was Tecumseh Park, 1877. The London Tecumsehs were playing Chicago. It was the thirteenth inning. Chicago was at bat, and there were men on base. A Chicago player knocked a fly deep into left field.

Several horses and carriages were parked there but Eddie Hornung . . . raced the pellet down to a point where it was falling into a phaeton. Hornung, with eyes on the ball, did not see the carriage until he was about to crash into it, but catching the whip-holder in his right hand, he threw himself into the phaeton and grabbed the ball with his left and saved the game for London.
(**London Centennial Review**, *1926*)

It was that kind of heroism that won the London Tecs the 1877 championship of the International Association, one of the first minor professinal leagues. That, and pitcher Fred Goldsmith's curve ball. Goldsmith is reputed to have invented the famous pitch.

When he sprung the curve ball, while with the Tecumseh team, he created the greatest confusion among opposing players and his work was an international sports sensation.
(**London Centennial Review**, *1926*)

Even allowing for some understandable hyperbole, 1877 was an exciting year for sports fans in London.

Baseball has been played in London parks since the 1850s. It was first played on the garrison cricket ground, now part of Victoria Park. Cricket was also very popular with the British soldiers and London's young men, as were boating, shooting, winter sports, hunting (the garrison kept a pack of hounds) and horse racing. As early as 1840, there were racket courts in London, and a gymnasium was set up by the officers of the garrison. The Tecumseh Boat Club was formed in the 1850s. The first bicycle appeared in 1869, and four years later the Forest City Riding Club was formed. The first regatta of the Forest City Rowing Club was held in 1879.

By the 1870s, the popularity of baseball had surpassed all other sports. The Morning Star Baseball Club, an amateur team, provided evidence of this; it was so named because the practises were held at 4:00 a.m., before the team members went to work!

By 1876, when the Tecumsehs went professional, their games were being played at the Fair Grounds (near Central and Richmond Streets). J. L. Englehart, an oil tycoon and president of the team, asked to be granted a portion of the old military reserve for use as a baseball park. A controversy, much coloured by ward politics, developed and dragged on for months. Englehart was so discouraged that he withdrew his application. The **Free Press** sports reporter commented bitterly:

A Bicycle Club meeting in Victoria Park, c. 1895.

A baseball poster, 1877.

A Baseball game at Tecumseh Park, Tecumsehs vs. Guelph Maple Leafs, June 21, 1877, from the Canadian Illustrated News.

Citizens of London will not thank small-souled aldermen or equally tight-laced ward politicians for their actions in compelling the managers of the Tecumsehs to purchase playing grounds outside the city limits but no other course was open to them.
(London Free Press, *April, 1877)*

A swampy river flat in London West was purchased by china merchant W. J. Reid, drained, laid out as a baseball diamond and named Tecumseh Park. According to the **Canadian Illustrated News,** the results were admirable.

The baseball grounds and buildings . . . have been fitted up at an expense of upwards of $3,000 and without doubt are the best for the purpose in the Dominion. Thousands of spectators visit the grounds whenever a match game takes place; in fact, on such occasions, everybody seems to give up business for baseball.
(Canadian Illustrated News, *July 14, 1877)*

In 1877, the team justified the expenditure on the grounds by winning the championship. But early in the 1878 season, the Tecs were accused of throwing a game. The **Free Press** warned sternly:

A few more games like yesterday and the managing directors, players as well as the umpire will have the entire seating accommodation and grounds for their exclusive benefit. The public is not blind to deception and cannot be imposed upon with impunity.
(London Free Press, *July 10, 1878)*

Although the Tecumsehs were temporarily out of favour, Tecumseh Park was not left ''for their exclusive benefit.'' Many teams have used it since 1878.

During the 1890s, the London Alerts played at Tecumseh Park as part of a small Canadian professional league. A brick-dust bicycle track was built and became the site of amateur and professional bicycle races. Annual diamond meets, at which the prizes were diamond rings, attracted top riders from across Canada and the United States. London's first moving picture was shown at Tecumseh Park after bicycle races held in 1895.

In the years before World War One, the London team of the Canadian Pro Baseball League used Tecumseh Park as their home field. During the twenties, it was the Michigan-Ontario Baseball League; London won the pennant in 1920, 1921 and 1922. After the Michigan-Ontario folded in 1925, the park was used

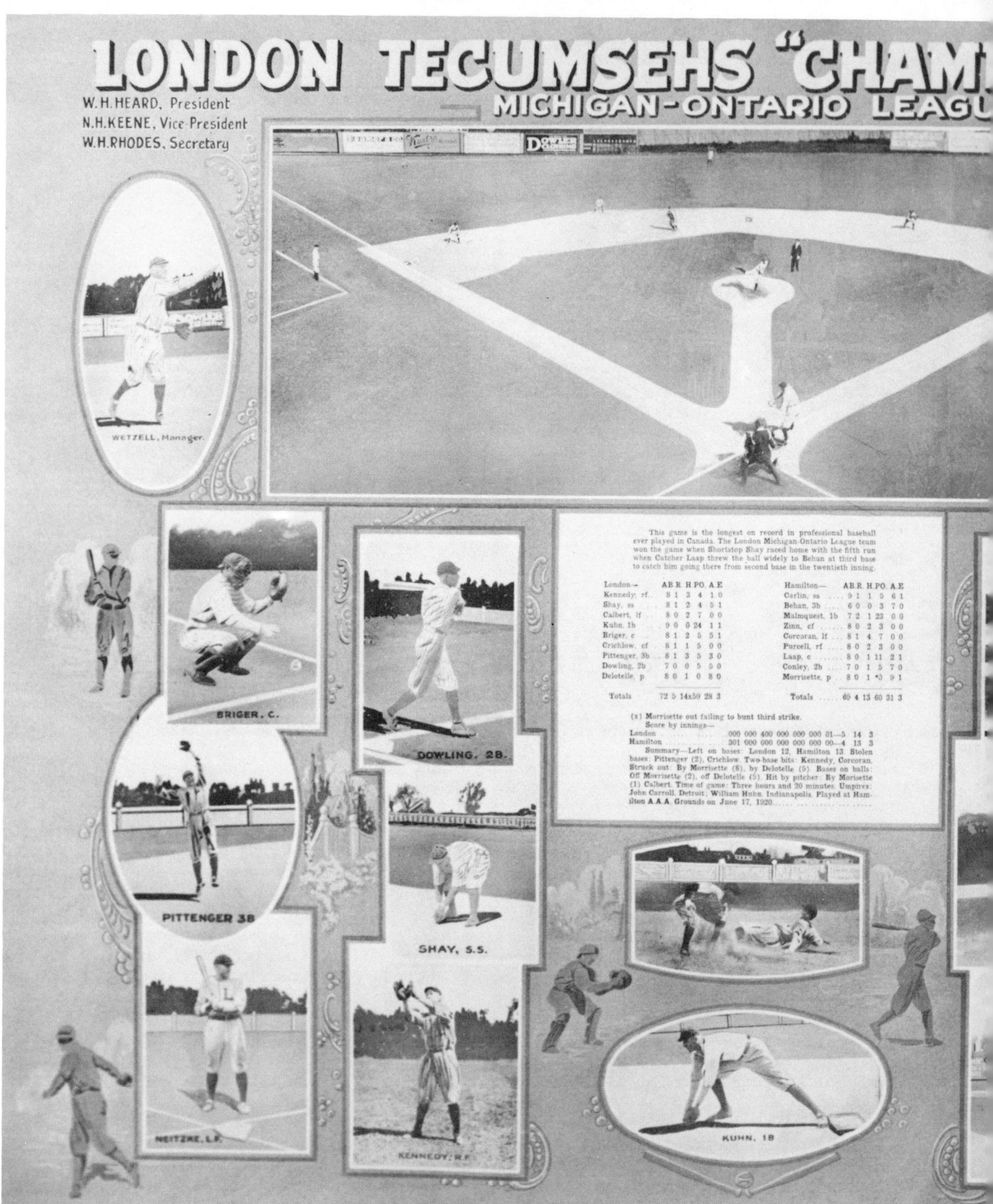

A Souvenir Poster of the 1920 Michigan-Ontario League Championship.

by amateur teams. In 1932, it was the site of a huge civic reception for "Silent Sandy," Sandy Somerville, the first Canadian golfer to win the U.S. amateur title.

Amateur baseball did not attract the crowds of the past, and by the mid-thirties the park was in financial difficulties. It was rescued by the Labatt family, who bought it in 1936 and donated it to the city, along with $10,000 for improvements. The flood of April 1937 swept away the existing grandstand, and a new grandstand and bleacher seats were built. The Pittsburgh Pirates operated a farm team in the Pony League at Labatt Park in 1940 and 1941. The Pirates installed floodlighting and made other improvements.

After the war, the park was home to the London Majors of the Inter-County League. The year 1948 was another great one in London baseball history; that year, the Majors won the Sandlot Baseball World Series.

London went baseball crazy last night! Citizens in all walks of life, right from Mayor George Wenige down to a ragged urchin . . . wanted to know how the Majors made out in the final game of the best-of-11 series with Fort Wayne. Majors 5, Fort Wayne 0, they were told . . .

"What a ball team, what a ball team!" the mayor enthused . . . "What a pitcher that Tommy White is. I think we should challenge the Cleveland Indians, or some other strong outfit. Boy, we really showed them how it's done, didn't we."

(**London Free Press,** *September 30, 1948*)

The Majors have played in the Inter-County League almost continuously since the 1940s, bringing home the League championship on several occasions.

Although Labatt Park is associated primarily with baseball, it has also accommodated football and soccer games, political rallies, boxing programs and many playground track meets like the one described below.

To the cheers and screams of more than 800 excited London children, the first half of the final Playgrounds track and field meet saw McMahen Park increase their lead over the eight other playgrounds . . . With some 400 contestants, the meet required as many as 10 events to be run off simultaneously and another full program tonight will be necessary to wind up the gigantic contest . . . Ranging in age from 8 years to 17, the youthful athletes showed a keen sense of fair play and sportsmanship in spite of an all-out effort by each playground to win.

(**London Free Press,** *August 27, 1947*)

Playgrounds have operated in London for over 80 years. As early as 1904, a group calling itself the Civic Improvement Society of London began asking the owners of vacant land to allow children to play on it. Parke Flats (later Thames Park) was hailed as the first public playground in Canada at its opening in June 1908. The London Playgrounds Association was organized by a group of prominent citizens inspired by Dr. Henry S. Curtis, an American recreation expert who visited London in 1912. The Association, funded by private donations, had soon hired a supervisor and set up three more programs in city schoolyards.

A Page from the P.U.C. Annual Report, 1922

In 1918, the Social Service Council approached council with a request for city-run playgrounds. The city put the question before the electorate on January 1, 1920. A few days before the vote, the following advertisement appeared:

Cities that lead the way in adopting modern ideas and meeting civic problems wisely and adequately are all found to be enthusiastic advocates of ample public playgrounds for children. London needs more playgrounds, where, under competent supervision our young folks — future citizens, remember — may play in SAFETY amid healthful surroundings, away from undesirable influences and companions — VOTE FOR PROGRESS!

(**London Free Press,** *December 26, 1919*)

Londoners voted for progress, and the program began that year in three parks, Thames, Queens and Birkett's Flats (in Chelsea Green). Baseball diamonds were laid out, basketball standards erected, and swings, teeters and maypoles were provided for the younger children. Male and female supervisors were placed in each playground.

In addition to basketball and baseball, volleyball, handicrafts, bicycle racing, archery, tennis, and football were all introduced over the next few years. Playground sports generated so much enthusiasm that the city's Chief Playgrounds Supervisor commented:

The interest was so keen this year that it was useless to send a person to umpire (playground baseball) unless he was thoroughly conversant with the rules and had the ability to handle not the players so much as the parents who came to cheer.

(**London Free Press,** *September, 1922*)

In 1920, there were no public swimming pools in London. Arrangements were made for boys from the playgrounds to use the Y.M.C.A. pool, and the Sulphur Baths pool was rented for a swim meet. By 1923, the situation had improved significantly. Thames Park pool was operative, two river swimming camps had been established and the P.U.C. had begun sponsoring swimming instruction. Three years later, when the Western Ontario Swimming Championships were held in London for the first time, swimming had become an integral part of the P.U.C. recreation program.

Another feature of the playground program in the 20s was the annual Festival, held at the end of August in Thames Park. In 1923, 1500 children participated in various exhibitions and sports, while 2000 proud parents looked on. In 1931, after a display of costumed folk dancing and gymnastic drills, the Playgrounds Supervisor commented smugly: ". . . This event I believe reflects the splendid training the children receive from the supervisors." Twilight swim and track meets also became regular events.

By 1929 the playgrounds' budget had doubled and there were 14 playgrounds in operation. According to E.V. Buchanan, the playgrounds were almost too popular with parents.

Last year we had a condition in the East End bordering on that of a creche. We had children brought down by their mothers, who wanted the supervisors to look after them, while they went down to the movies . . . While I am a firm believer in the community playground movement and believe that it may be made to pay dividends in community health, I am coming to doubt whether it is not having a psychological effect on the parents, which is perhaps not entirely a benefit.

(**London Free Press,** *January 17, 1929*)

Recreation programs were not designed simply to occupy children's idle hours, but to build character, as this excerpt from the Chief Playground Supervisor's report reflects:

What is the result of this expenditure of time and money? Are the citizens of London getting any return for their investment? . . . There is no doubt that we are succeeding in our endeavor to create in children the proper spirit of play. To lay the foundation for a full and splendid manhood or womanhood is our first consideration.

(**P.U.C. Annual Report,** *1929*)

Oblivious to these serious goals, London children enjoyed the programs. During the 30s, interest in track and field events increased, partly as a result of the good Canadian showing at the 1929 Olympics. As the Depression deepened, there was little money for recreation programs but some playgrounds were kept open.

During the 1940s, the P.U.C. began to organize men's softball teams, the first step towards a complete adult recreation program. In 1945, the Recreation Supervisor wrote: "With so many people making use of the recreation areas it may be rightfully assumed that these areas are contributing materially to the wholesome recreation and welfare of London citizens in all age groups."

During the 50s and 60s, the recreation program continued to expand and diversify. Community Centres and seniors programs were introduced, and pools and playgrounds were added to serve newly annexed areas. Artificial ice surfaces and later, skating arenas extended the winter season. By the late 60s, recreation programs for all ages were offered throughout the year and the Free Press could report:

London's recreational program may fairly be described in superlatives. In resources and participation there is probably nothing quite as attractive within a comparative population area anywhere in Canada.

(**London Free Press,** *July 15, 1968*)

There are now over 40,000 children in year-round P.U.C. programs, over 10,000 adults and seniors in year-round general interest programs, and almost 700 adult sports teams. Londoners who have come to take these excellent facilities and programs for granted should perhaps recall the words of Thomas Adams, the famous urban planner, who wrote in 1922:

The most beneficial change recorded in the social life of London was when its citizens had recreation and outdoor sport organized for them. These provided them with counter attractions to the saloon. Now that the saloon has gone the recreation facilities are even more needed.

The "Queen" of Pottersburg, a participant in an early playground pageant, c. 1930.

PUTTING DOWN ROOTS — CONCLUSION

In 1951, London had 750 acres of parkland, The total is now almost 2800 acres. Despite concerns that the parks system is not keeping pace with development, London seems singularly blessed.

One of the most significant developments of the 1960s was a joint purchase plan with the Upper Thames River Conservation Authority, which has given Londoners access to many acres of riverside lands, and led to the creation of a bikeway linking the city's existing river parks.

Generous donations continue to add to London's green space. Developer Mowbray Sifton's gift of a large portion of the Byron Bog (now the Sifton Botanical Bog) in 1962 helped preserve what zoologist Dr. W.W. Judd has called "a living museum of unique plants." The Harris family, in addition to donating "Eldon House" as a city museum, gave its lovely riverside grounds for a park, now the site of the popular Hot Air Balloon Fiesta. The most recent major donation was Meadowlily Woods, a 150-acre parcel of land in southeast London, the bequest of London lawyer Harrison Fraser.

The five percent provision of the Ontario Planning Act requires developers to dedicate a portion of newly subdivided land for recreational purposes. The P.U.C. may choose to take the land, or a money payment, which is put in a fund reserved for future parkland acquisitions. The 'five percent provision' ensures that London's rapidly growing suburbs will have open spaces.

Londoners have continued to fight for their parks, often in a David-and-Goliath battle with developers.

In 1969, when a local church offered to buy the Broughdale Lands, an empty floodplain on the north branch of the Thames at Richmond Street, a heated controversy developed over whether to allow the land to be developed or to keep it as a park. Local residents made a strong case for keeping the land open, with the result that C.J.F. Ross Park was created, an important link in the growing chain of river parks.

In 1970, residents of North London opposed a move by St. Joseph's Hospital to build a parking garage on Doidge Park, despite assurances that the park would be re-created on the roof of the garage. The hospital was eventually forced to build elsewhere. In 1977, residents of the Whitehills area protested plans to run a storm sewer through Foxhollow Park, a natural ravine in the area. Although the sewer project went ahead, the city responded to the concerns by ensuring that the landscape was restored to a near-natural state.

One of the most unusual natural areas in London, rivalling the Sifton Bog for the variety of plant and animal life, is the Westminster Ponds/Pond Mills area. W.E. Saunders, a famous naturalist, owned property around the ponds and built a cabin there in 1920. He and fellow members of the McIlwraith Field Naturalists sought to have the ponds designated as a bird sanctuary as early as 1923, and efforts to preserve the ponds have continued to the present day. During the 1970's, the Upper Thames River Conservation Authority and the city began a joint program of acquisition and conservation in the Pond Mills area. At the same time, however, a major residential development began, creating a situation fraught with potential conflict. Concerned citizens recently lost a hard-fought battle to preserve Matthews Woods, another section of Pond Mills now slated for development.

New parks continue to be created. London's newest park, Piccadilly Park, has much in common with its oldest. Both were part of the British military reserve (as the original stone marker in the northeast corner of Piccadilly Park attests) and both were transformed from neglected eyesores to attractive green spaces in response to public demand.

London has an enviable parks system, with a long and colourful history. From the friendliness of a neighbourhood park to the grandeur of Springbank, Londoners care deeply about these patches of green and blue in an increasingly colourless urban landscape.

Parks are not only desirable from the point of view of creating an amenity for the enjoyment of the citizens. In the modern city, they are essential for the preservation of city life.
(**Report on Town Planning Survey of the City of London,** *Thomas Adams, 1922*)

"Spring Bank Landing", one of twelve views of London sold as a souvenir of the Fair of 1882. Note the look-out at the top of the hill, and the steamer at left.

Installing Electric Pumps and Motors, Springbank, 1911
— E.V. Buchanan is at the right. His companions are not identified.

BIBLIOGRAPHY

This is a partial list of the published sources consulted in preparing this book.

Adams, Thomas. **Report on Town Planning Survey of the City of London, April-May 1922.**

Andreae, Christopher. **The Industrial Heritage of London and Area.** London, Ontario: Ontario Society for Industrial Archaeology in conjunction with London Historical Museums, 1984.

Armstrong, Frederick H. **The Forest City, An Illustrated History of London, Canada.** Windsor, Ontario: Windsor Publications, 1986.

Bremner, Archie, **City of London Ontario, Canada, The Pioneer Period and the London of To-day.** London, Ontario: London Printing and Lithographing Company, 1900. (Reprinted by the London Public Library Board, 1967)

Buchanan, E.V. **London's Water Supply, A History,** London, Ontario: London Public Utilities Commission, 1968.

Buchanan, E.V. **Roses in December, An Autobiography.** London, Ontario: Galt House, 1986.

Curnoe, Glen, W. **The London and Port Stanley Railway, 1915-1965 A Picture History.**

Dolan, T.J. **Twenty Years of Conservation on the Upper Thames Watershed.** Stratford: Upper Thames River Conservation Authority, 1967.

Duff, Robert. **London Parks and Recreation, 1871-1973: A History of the Recreation Department, Public Utilities Commission.** London, Ontario: P.U.C., 1973.

Hilts, Stewart G. Ed. **Natural Areas in London, Ontario: Towards an Appreciation.** London, Ontario: Department of Geography, 1977.

Judd, W.W. **Early Naturalists and Natural History Societies of London, Ontario:** London, Ontario: Phelps Publishing, 1979.

Lutman, John H. **The Historic Heart of London,** London, Ontario: Corporation of the City of London, 1977, 1978.

Lutman, John H. **The South and the West.** London, Ontario: Corporation of the City of London, 1979.

McTaggart, Kenneth D. **The Victoria Day Disaster** London, Ontario: McTaggart, 1978.

Miller, Orlo. **A Century of Western Ontario.** Toronto: The Ryerson Press, 1949.

Proctor, Redfern, Bousfield, Bacon, **City of London Parks and Recreation Study.** Toronto, Ontario: Proctor, Redfern, Bousfield, Bacon, 1964.

Prothero, Frank and Nancy. **Port Stanley: Musings and Memories.** Port Stanley, Ontario: Nan-Sea Publications, 1980.

Spicer, Elizabeth, ed. **Descriptions of London and Its Environs 1799-1854.** Occasional Paper #XVII, London Public Library and Art Museum.

St-Denis Guy. **Byron: Pioneer Days in Westminster Township.** Lambeth, Ontario: Crinklaw Press, 1985.

Tausky, Nancy Z. and Lynne D. DiStefano. **Victorian Architecture in London and Southwestern Ontario, Symbols of Aspiration.** Toronto, Ontario: University of Toronto Press, 1986.

Upper Thames Valley Conservation Report, 1952. (Summary) Toronto, Ontario: Queen's Printer, 1952.

Other research materials included newspapers and newspaper clippings, and P.U.C. Annual Reports.

The north branch of the Thames, Blackfriar's Bridge and London West from Ridout Street, c. 1870.

The north branch of the River Thames with Thornwood, the Becher residence on the left, and Becher's Island, later Gibbon's Park, on the right, c. 1880.

ISBN 0-919549-17-9

Stonehouse Publications
17 Queen Street, St. Catharines, Ontario L2R 5G5
Telephone (416) 684-7251